The Audacity of Despotism: How The U.S. Liberal Mainstream Media Tried
to Swing the 2016 Presidential Election and Failed

by Paige Donner

Table of Contents

Preface

It's time we take back our hijacked mainstream media, America.

As Americans we have a right to be outraged by how the U.S. liberal mainstream media attempted to hack our 2016 presidential election. Liberal mainstream media's relentless bullying and attacks during the 2016 presidential campaign cycle on the conservative candidate, now President Trump, was nothing less than a pack of wolves going after its chosen prey.

As an American citizen who veers more towards the side of conservative thinking, I have an inalienable right to feel disgusted by the liberal media's unwavering torpedoing of one political party's candidate, namely the Republican candidate. Doing so was, and is, an attack not just on freedom of speech and the 4th Estate's original nonpartisan watchdog role, but also on freedom of thought and on a free citizenry's fundamental, constitutional First Amendment rights. How so? Because focused reporting on real issues, like jobs, the economy, middle-America's mass opioid addiction, future immigration policies, education, the country's failing infrastructure and so forth were sacrificed in favor of sensationalist, click-bait headlines. Click-bait headlines do nothing to move a substantive dialogue forward and in fact are designed to obfuscate the truly relevant issues at hand.

For tyranny to prevail, a government requires the co-operation of its handmaidens of mass media. A co-opted 4th Estate paves the way for despotism to flourish. Many of us Americans have felt for years that we were being manipulated and force-fed horse manure through our liberal mainstream media channels, most of which are corporate owned. Moreover, many of those channels that are not corporate owned are financed largely through the serpentine holdings of a left-leaning billionaire financier, namely George Soros. This point is investigated and illustrated in detail in this book. Thanks largely to the then-candidate, now our President Trump, the 2016 election put this undeniable failing of our mainstream media under a microscope. The media got it wrong. The media failed to report the facts in a non-partisan manner. And most importantly, the media completely missed – or simply ignored – the pulse of the nation, the pulse of the American people.

And that isn't the only way in which American citizens have been failed. Living in the politically correct, mainstream media-induced climate of groupthink that led up to what every liberal media outlet predicted would be the coronation of the Democratic candidate has even more ominous significance: Americans no longer felt they were free to have and voice their own true opinions.

For an American citizen, home of the free, land of the brave, this is not just blasphemous, it's a sacrilege.

Case in point: There are two main reasons why the majority of the political polls got this 2016 presidential election so wrong so consistently. 1. Because the liberal mainstream media were reporting statistics based on skewed samplings of the population (in other words, purposeful manipulation of data in order to persuade the American citizenry of a wished-for, constructed outcome, i.e. that Hillary would win) and 2. Because Americans, when polled by telephone, were afraid to say what they really thought and felt – namely that they were voting Trump.

That this climate of fear, groupthink and thought police existed to such a high degree in our country leading up to the 2016 election is cause for more than just concern. It calls for outrage. As American citizens we have an inalienable, constitutional right - and duty - to not just think independently and freely but also to speak our minds freely and independently, without fear of reprisals.

It's time we take back our media.

It's time we take back our media from politically motivated puppet masters and demand that it serves its original intended purpose: to hold power accountable in an unbiased, non-partisan manner.

Media, like government, is here to serve the people. It's not here to control the population. And it's certainly not here to impose its NY/ LA -hatched codes of elitist beliefs on the rest of the country.

Mainstream liberal media over this past decade became handmaidens to a government run by an Executive Office that was on the path toward tyranny.

As American citizens, we need to take back our government, re-assert ourselves in our media, and make our country great again.

Beware of Facebook

If you're primarily getting your news from *Facebook, Huffington Post* and *Buzzfeed*, beware! These vectors of fake news, along with *CNN*, are not there to serve an informed citizenry. They are there to doctor up stories to fuel the agendas of the dwindling power structure of the liberal left culture tyrants. Contrary to what the mainstream media has been blasting from its bully pulpits since the historic 2016 presidential win of Donald Trump, the majority of published news stories on Facebook is not from micro "alt-right" sites but by well-funded and well-greased media machines such as *The Huffington Post* and the *New York Times*. *The Huffington Post* itself boasts of being the largest news publisher on Facebook.

Getting your news primarily from Facebook is like drinking a bottle of coke every day and thinking you're getting your recommended daily allowance of vitamins and nutrients. Cola, as most everyone knows, is filled with sugar, chemicals, caffeine and food coloring. It's hardly a diet on which to base a healthy lifestyle. Similarly, *FB, Buzzfeed, CNN* et al. are not filled solely with news items or facts that are meant to inform a responsible citizenry, but rather to sway people towards a prescribed mindset. So, just as you wouldn't fill up on only sugar, caffeine, chemicals and food coloring, so shouldn't we be feeding our minds the intellectual equivalent. That is, not if we want to continue to be free Americans - responsible to our duties as American citizens - which include being an informed member of the electorate.

4

Investing in Freedom

What's called for is investing in yourself. This isn't the place nor the time – nor the book – for dietary recommendations. But it is an appropriate place to highlight the importance of subscribing to a variety of worthy news outlets. This book mentions a good many of the legitimate news sources that offer a balancing perspective to mainstream liberal media: *Breitbart, Newsmax, Investor's Business Daily*, the *Palm Beach Group*, the *Wall Street Journal, Consortium News, the Drudge Report, Rush Limbaugh*, and *Fox News* along with others. With several of these media outlets under threat of advertisers pulling their dollars, or even recently experiencing ad dollars being pulled as a form of retaliation for reporting news stories without the prevalent liberal mainstream media bias, now has never been a better time to become a paid subscriber.

For the cost of a cup of coffee, you can get your monthly news and coverage from sources you can trust and which offer multiple perspectives. Your initial response might be, well, Facebook gives me all that for free. But it's not free, not when the cost of that free information is having your head filled with falsities at best and brainwashing at worst. Mainstream liberal media, the kind most highly trafficked on platforms like Facebook, is stripping us of the ability and fortitude to think independently while it pummels us with groupthink and cultural despotism. Mainstream liberal media has become our modern day thought police. And the liberal culture tyrants who run it are its masters.

Moreover, the discussion as to whether Facebook should or shouldn't, will or won't, fact-check their news stories is irrelevant. If they do finally decide to fact-check their news stories then we, as information consumers, have just handed over the keys to the Truth Kingdom to a behemoth whose sole purpose is to show a profit to its investors every year. Because one thing Facebook never purported to be was a "watchdog of the powerful," as was the original mission of pure news organizations. This book delves into this nuanced point in greater detail and illustrates how established and "trusted" fact-checking sites, such as *Snopes*, can label a story false or true based on superficial evaluation and arbitrary judgment.

Paying for what is of value – factual news and information – is the best way to protect against a liberal media that continues to attempt to hijack the democratic process and brainwash the minds of the American citizenry. There is no price too high for freedom. Our fathers, sons, brothers, uncles and grandfathers, along with some of our mothers, sisters, aunts and daughters, have fought and died to keep America a free country. Paying a few bucks each month to several of your chosen news sources in order to have above-the-board, factual news reporting at your fingertips is a very small price to pay for freedom.

- Paige Donner, *Paris*, January 19, 2017

Introduction

This is about the future of democracy   (article title, *USA Today Opinion, page 10A,*
November 10, 2016)

The meltdown in our U.S. Media that we witnessed during this 2016 presidential election cycle calls
for immediate, unwavering and unflinching scrutiny.

That the mainstream liberal and so-called "centrist non-partisan" corporate media outlets consistently
miscalled the election results and misreported the pulse of the American electorate all the way up
through the last hours of the final election tally of the early morning on November 9th 2016 bear
witness to the fact that we no longer have a free and independent, non-partisan media acting as the
fourth estate and government watchdog in our great nation.

As a member of the media, the Trump supporter alone in my flock of fellow media "elites," all of
whom vocally supported liberals, democrats, independents and the Clinton Camp, I faced daily derision
all throughout the U.S. Presidential election campaign. Suffice it to say that when the Paris-based
international foreign journalists and correspondents hosted their Food Lovers for Hillary event in
September 2016, I was not on the invite list. I was the *only one* in my so-called tribe of media-elites –
99% of whom are liberal leaning here in Paris – who was not invited. When people talk now about the
echo chamber among the liberals, I know firsthand wherefrom they speak. Being painted as a loony by
your colleagues, peers and contemporaries just for holding a differing opinion and maintaining a
perspective apart from your peer-circle majority's, is not pleasant.

And it has profound professional and even social consequences.

When *USA Today*, my employer, came out with their editorial board's statement at the end of
September 2016 admonishing Americans to not vote for Trump and painting him as "unfit for
president," I knew that I was backed into a corner in terms of my professional standing.

In the past 12 months, a time span corresponding to my vocal support of Trump as a candidate, my
assignments were cut from 30+ articles a month to 10. Articles that I submitted by deadline and ready
for print, have now been backlogged for 12 months, queued for publishing (but not published) for 12
months and more at this time of writing. I had been working for Gannett/ *USA Today* for 2 solid years
prior to this as the sole designated permalance contributor from Paris. At the time I publicly jumped on
the Trump bandwagon I had had dozens of articles published by them, all adhering to the regular time

frame of monthly or weekly deadlines. My publish dates were always within days of assignment submission.

My assignment editor, based in McLean, VA. did not reply to any of my emails for 10 months leading up to the presidential election. At time of writing, two weeks after the successful presidential campaign of our 45th president of the United States, Donald Trump, I have just now received a reply. Her response to why my articles have not been published is that there has been a backlog and that the assigned editor will get to them by rank of priority.

During the 2 years I worked for *USA Today* leading up to the primaries of this presidential cycle my articles were always, and I use that word conscientiously, always, published within 72 hours maximum of my submitting them. For the 12 month period leading up to the election of Donald Trump, during which I was a vocal supporter both in conversation and on social media, my pay as earned from *USA Today* dropped 300%. In other words, during my support of my chosen political candidate, a political candidate that it turned out was not just disproved of by my employer's editorial board but was publicly put in print on our Opinion page as being "unfit for the presidency," – signed off on by *USA Today's* entire editorial board – my rate of pay was reduced to 1/4th of what it previously was during the first 2 ½ years I worked for this U.S. media giant.

If my personal experience is any indication as to what a member of the media risks in today's climate of liberal-ethos bullying and elite, clubby echo chambers, then the reprisals are quantitative and severe. To put it bluntly, in the vestiges of what remained of our once-exalted U.S. Fourth Estate leading up to the election of our 45th President of the United States, a conservative-leaning journalist working for a liberal-leaning, but previously non-partisan, national news outlet could expect ostracism, pay cuts, work cuts and marginalization – irrespective of job performance.

And the derision suffered at the hands of my peers whose caustic wits and incisive criticisms are never so eloquently expressed than when directed towards one of their own who happens to hold a differing opinion, is telling. It is telling of the bullying mentality that permeates our liberal media structures and offers an insight as to how it spread so virally and so successfully during these past 10 years, corresponding to the prolific rise and dominance of digital and social media throughout the two terms of the Obama administration.

And these are just the facts.

As a member of the media and a Trump supporter I would like to offer readers a glimpse into what it's like to be a member of the "elite media" tribe, but one who holds conservative-leaning, often unpopular viewpoints, among my so-called tribe, the vast majority of whom are decidedly liberal-leaning.

In a peer group who was overwhelmingly not Trump supporters in the 2016 presidential election campaign cycle, holding steadfast to my political views as a working member of corporate media often felt like being the lore sheep among packs of vitriolic, mud-slinging wolves during this past run-up to the 2016 U.S. Presidential Election. Suffice it to say, I really never was interested in hearing that speculative conversation about the size of our President's, er, hands.

As one of the "others," and one whose opinions and viewpoints in fact seem to correspond with millions of other Americans', Americans who did not find a champion for themselves in the form of a corporate media personality during the elections of 2016, I feel it is useful to share my insights. These insights will attempt to shed light on this now much-ballyhooed subject of the insular elite media echo chamber.

Furthermore, by presenting dozens of articles and editorials by said elite media liberals from during, pre-, and post-election cycle, I will present a framework as to how and why this professional peer group pressure to "fall in line" with the dominant opinion/viewpoint exists today within the clubby elite media circles - circles that are overwhelmingly liberal-minded - and how this mechanism of intolerance and the propensity towards being "thought police" is putting the future of America's democracy in peril today.

This insight also helps explain why and how President Trump himself emerged as the popular media champion for his supporters, supporters that number in the tens of millions of Americans all across the nation. Trump as a corporate popular media champion is a phrase many will find paradoxical. But, when you define his corporate platform as the technology platform known as Twitter and the notion of "popular" in that his approach was and is to communicate directly, unfiltered, to his multiple millions of followers, then this re-casting of the definition of media champion holds water.

Chapter 1

Watchdogs of The Powerful – The Historical Role of Political Journalists

A nation of sheep will beget a government of wolves.

– Edward R. Murrow

"It is commonly acknowledged throughout society that to have real democracy it is important to have a level of transparency in government, meaning that the public can see what the government does in the public's name.

One way to achieve this transparency is to have an independent watchdog, paying attention to and informing the public on what the government does. This is the idea that the term 'The Fourth Estate' comes from." - *The Fourth Estate* – Essay by Stuart Pirie

Source: https://www.booksie.com/posting/stuart-pirie/the-fourth-estate-265117#k3kxpkDZooZiPYHc.99

AUTHOR: The following analyses, written in 2007 and 2008, offer insight into the state of media affairs in Great Britain and ask the pointed questions as to whether a Fourth Estate even exists any longer?

In the U.S.'s current state of affairs in regards to its media, this same question will yield similar analyses and, I would argue, a similar conclusion: That the Fourth Estate, as it was first developed and defined, no longer exists today in the United States, at least in any semblance of its original form and function.

To follow my line of reasoning, lets look at the following missives and how the concept of the Fourth Estate was first established and what its intended function in society initially was:

Driving Democracy, Harvard Kennedy School, Chapter 8 "The Fourth Estate" 2007 pgs 1 & 2

Source: https://www.hks.harvard.edu/fs/pnorris/Acrobat/Driving%20Democracy/Chapter%208.pdf

(This following passage is taken from the above-noted source) -
Liberal theorists have long argued that the existence of an unfettered and independent press within each nation is essential in the process of democratization, by contributing towards the right of freedom of expression, thought and conscience, strengthening the responsiveness and accountability of governments to all citizens, and providing a pluralist platform and channel of political expression for a multiplicity of groups and interests.

The guarantee of freedom of expression and information is recognized as a basic human right in the Universal Declaration of Human Rights adopted by the UN in 1948, the European Convention on Human Rights, the American Convention on Human Rights, and the African Charter on Human and Peoples' Rights.

In particular, Article 19 of the **1948 Universal Declaration of Human Rights** states:

> "Everyone has the right to freedom of opinion and expression; this right includes freedom to hold opinions without interference and to seek, receive and impart information and ideas through any media and regardless of frontiers."

James D. Wolfensen echoed these sentiments when he was the president of the World Bank: "A free press is not a luxury. A free press is at the absolute core of equitable development, because if you cannot enfranchise poor people, if they do not have a right to expression, if there is no searchlight on corruption and inequitable practices, you cannot build the public consensus needed to bring about change." *Driving Democracy* – Chapter 8 9/15/2007

AUTHOR: It is essential to remember that in the prior 8 years (at time of this writing December 2016), throughout the Obama administration, the press and whistleblowers, which in essence are what investigative journalists are, suffered legal, monetary, career and even physical body reprisals for doing their jobs diligently.

This 2014 article in *Mother Jones* acknowledges the degree to which our 1ˢᵗ Amendment has been brought under attack:

Whistleblower Crackdowns, Self-Censorship, Stonewalled FOIAs: The 1st Amendment Under Attack , by Peter Van Buren, *Mother Jones*, June 2014
Source: http://www.motherjones.com/politics/2014/06/first-amendment-free-speech-attack

The First Amendment

"Congress shall make no law respecting an establishment of religion, or prohibiting the free exercise thereof; or abridging the freedom of speech, or of the press; or the right of the people peaceably to assemble, and to petition the Government for a redress of grievances."

The First Amendment was meant to make one thing indisputably clear: free speech was the basis for a government of the people. Without a free press, as well as the ability to openly gather, debate, protest, and criticize, how would the people be able to judge their government's adherence to the other rights? How could people vote knowledgeably if they didn't know what was being done in their name by their government? An informed citizenry, Thomas Jefferson stated, was "a vital requisite for our survival as a free people." ...

Sealed Lips and the Whistleblower

All government agencies have regulations requiring employees to obtain permission before speaking to the representatives of the people—that is, journalists. The US Intelligence Community has among the most restrictive of these policies, banning employees and contractors completely from talking with the media without prior authorization. Even speaking about unclassified information is a no-no that may cost you your job. A government ever more in lockdown mode has created what one journalist calls a culture where censorship is the norm.

So who does speak to Americans about their government? Growing hordes of spokespeople, communications staff, trained PR crews, and those anonymous senior officials who pop up so regularly in news articles in major papers.

With the government obsessively seeking to hide or spin what it does, in-the-sunlight contact barred, and those inside locked behind an iron curtain of secrecy, the whistleblower has become the paradigmatic figure of the era. Not surprisingly, anyone who blows a whistle has, in these years, come under fierce attack.

Pick a case: Tom Drake exposing early NSA efforts to turn its spy tools on Americans, Edward Snowden proving that the government has us under constant surveillance, Chelsea Manning documenting war crimes in Iraq and sleazy diplomacy everywhere, John Kiriakou acknowledging torture by his former employer the CIA, or Robert MacLean revealing Transportation Safety Administration malfeasance. In each instance, the threat of jail was quick to surface. The nuclear option against such truthtellers is the Espionage Act, a law that offended the Constitution when implemented in the midst of World War I. It has been resurrected by the Obama administration as a blunt wartime tool for silencing and punishing whistleblowers.

The Obama administration has already **charged** six **people** under that act for allegedly mishandling classified information. Even Richard Nixon only invoked it once, in a failed prosecution against Pentagon Papers whistleblower Daniel Ellsberg.

Indeed, the very word espionage couldn't be stranger in the context of these cases. None of those charged spied. None sought to aid an enemy or make money selling secrets. No matter. In Post-Constitutional America, the powers-that-be stand ready to twist language in whatever Orwellian direction is necessary to bridge the gap between reality and the king's needs.

Driving Democracy, Harvard Kennedy School, Chapter 8 "The Fourth Estate" 2007 pg. 4
Source: https://www.hks.harvard.edu/fs/pnorris/Acrobat/Driving%20Democracy/Chapter%208.pdf

The role of journalists as watchdogs of the powerful
In their 'watchdog' role, the channels of the news media can function to promote government transparency, accountability, and public scrutiny of decision-makers in power, by highlighting policy failures, maladministration by public officials, corruption in the judiciary, and scandals in the corporate sector.

Since Edmund Burke, the 'fourth estate' has traditionally been regarded as one of the classic checks and balances in the division of powers. Investigative journalism can open the government's record to external scrutiny and critical evaluation, and hold authorities accountable for their actions, whether public sector institutions, non-profit organizations, or private companies.

AUTHOR: One of the main points to underscore in the above passage is that investigative journalism, when it does finally successfully gain access to public records, can "open the government to external scrutiny and evaluation." The key being gaining access. The highly publicized *New York Times* legal battle with the highly politicized Obama justice department to protect its journalist's source dragged on for 7 years, meaning all the way through June 2015, before it was finally ruled that he (the NYT journalist) would not be made to testify and reveal his sources.

This is what the *New York Times* had to say when that Justice Department ruling finally came in:

Times Reporter Will Not Be Called To Testify In Leak Case, by Matt Apuzzo, *New York Times,* January 12, 2015
Source: http://www.nytimes.com/2015/01/13/us/times-reporter-james-risen-will-not-be-called-to-testify-in-leak-case-lawyers-say.html?_r=0

Mr. Risen, a two-time Pulitzer Prize winner, was the highest-profile journalist drawn into the Obama administration's attempt to crack down on government officials who talk to reporters about national security. The Justice Department has brought more charges in leak cases than were brought in all previous administrations combined. The case became a rallying cry for journalism groups and civil rights advocates. Mr. Risen took his fight to the Supreme Court and lost, but Attorney General Eric H. Holder Jr. ultimately said prosecutors would not force him to reveal his sources.

"We said from the very beginning that under no circumstances would Jim identify confidential sources to the government or anyone else," Mr. Risen's lawyer, Joel Kurtzberg, said. "The significance of this goes beyond Jim Risen. It affects journalists everywhere. Journalists need to be able to uphold that confidentiality in order to do their jobs."

AUTHOR: At what point does the media establishment bend to the powers that be? Of course the publishers and editorial boards of our biggest media establishments would say, Never. At least that is what they would say in public. But what kind of collusion is reached behind closed doors? What kind of deal making goes on with highly politicized justice departments, the kind we saw during the Obama administration, in order to maintain the façade of an impartial news media? One whose mission it is to educate, keep informed and mobilize the public at large. Indeed, whose mission it is is to be a government watchdog.

The Fourth Estate – Essay by Stuart Pirie
Source: https://www.booksie.com/posting/stuart-pirie/the-fourth-estate-265117#k3kxpkDZooZiPYHc.99

Once again Coronel's article, *The Role of The Media in Deepening Democracy* (2003), mentions this point: 'Democracy requires the active participation of citizens. Ideally, the media should keep citizens engaged in the business of governance by informing, educating and mobilizing the public.'

It is commonly acknowledged throughout society that to have real democracy it is important to have a level of transparency in government, meaning that the public can see what the government does in the public's name. One way to achieve this transparency is to have an independent watchdog, paying attention to and informing the public on what the government does. This is the idea that the term 'The Fourth Estate' comes from.

Following on from the 19th century and with the growing influence and power of the press it led to the 'nickname' of 'The Fourth Estate' who's power and influence over political and public life was considered significant. The three 'estates' being 'watched' by the press (the fourth) were the House of Lords, The House of Commons and the Church.

Unofficially, the job of the Fourth Estate was to act as a watchdog for the public over these three 'estates' meaning that the press at the time of the Fourth Estate's conception and also today, had huge influence over public and political life. When discussing the historical emergence of the concept of the Fourth Estate it is also important to analyze to what extent the concept of the Fourth Estate is still useful for understanding the role of the press today. With this in mind it is important to attempt to answer questions such as: does the idea of the Fourth Estate still exist and in relation to this, what role does the press play today?

...It is also essential to try and answer the question 'Does the Fourth Estate still exist?' Coronel's example of the media using its influence over the public and political life to disrupt corrupt presidencies and governments suggests that to some extent the Fourth Estate does still exist.

'...in independent and democratic countries, the free press encourages government responsiveness to public concerns...' (Norris, P. , *Driving Democracy*, 2008)

Bearing Norris' thoughts in mind, we must now ask, does the press in this country encourage government responsiveness to public concerns...? Before answering that question it is important to mention that there is significant outrage towards the government...

Along with this there is little responsiveness to public concerns by the government, meaning that our press in Britain does not encourage government responsiveness to public concerns. This leads to the conclusion, based on Norris' thoughts about democratic countries, that we no longer live in a democratic country and therefore there is an argument to be made that the Fourth Estate no longer exists here.

Chapter 2

The Insidious Hoax of An Impartial U.S. News Media

> We have currently a built-in allergy to unpleasant or disturbing information. Our mass media reflect this. But unless we get up off our fat surpluses and recognize that television in the main is being used to distract, delude, amuse, and insulate us, then television and those who finance it, those who look at it, and those who work at it, may see a totally different picture too late.
> —Edward R. Murrow

Why Independent Media?

Source: https://www.democracynow.org/about

For true democracy to work, people need easy access to independent, diverse sources of news and information.

But the last two decades have seen unprecedented corporate media consolidation. The U.S. media was already fairly homogeneous in the early 1980s: some fifty media conglomerates dominated all media outlets, including television, radio, newspapers, magazines, music, publishing and film.

In the year 2000, just *six* corporations dominated the U.S. media.

In addition, corporate media outlets in the U.S. are legally responsible to their shareholders to maximize profits.

AUTHOR: To get your daily dose of news and punditry in the United States you watch *Fox News* if you're conservative-leaning and *MSNBC, CNN* and *Bloomberg* if you're left-leaning. For a short while the myth prevailed that *CNN* was the "neutral" station. The myth was so convincing to the masses that here in Paris – where I am writing this cultural observation of my own country, America – the recent 2016 US Presidential Election Night festivities were set to institutionally propagate this myth. How so?

For the first time in our centuries' long history of friendship, the French government, in the form of their state-owned and operated *Maison de la Radio France,* offered to host an all-night event of festivities tracking the U.S. Election on big screens and offering Texas bbq and hot dogs for the 1000+ revelers expected to show up.

In past election years, the Democrats Abroad and Republicans Overseas have always, without exception, co-hosted an event here in Paris at which interested parties could attend and support their candidates. It was always a very civil affair, notwithstanding high-running emotions, no doubt because the American expat community here in Paris is still a relatively small one and paths are frequently crossed.

This year, the French socialist government decided to take matters into their own hands and host an event that would include, by mandate, both the members of Republicans Overseas and Democrats Abroad as well as allow for several hundred (+600) members of the general public to attend this all-night event of firsthand, albeit remote, observation of a U.S. Presidential Election.

The initial agreement between Democrats Abroad, Republicans Overseas and the *Maison de la Radio France* stipulated that streaming media coverage was to be provided by both *CNN* and *Fox News*. These were the outlets for the real-time news reporting that would be broadcast on big screens throughout the gigantic venue located on Avenue President Kennedy in Paris' 16th Arrondissement.

Two weeks before the event, the *Maison de la Radio* contacted representatives of Democrats Abroad and Republicans Overseas via telephone and informed them that subsequent to an exclusive deal that the *Maison de la Radio France* had just signed with *CNN*, it would no longer be providing streaming coverage by *Fox News* on Election Night at the event. The thousand plus invitations had already been sent out.

During the normal monthly Republicans Overseas meeting at the end of October, this just-developing update was discussed. That day's copy of *USA Today* ran several headlining election-related stories, one stating that the RNC had definitively disavowed President Trump; and another about the leaked Donna Brazile emails clearly proving that, before the debates, she had slipped Candidate Hillary the debate questions from the *CNN*-moderated election debate that she had hosted for the network. Hence, the subsequently dubbed *Clinton News Network.*

The *Maison de la Radio France's* argument that *CNN* was the "neutral" network providing reasoned and impartial commentary and coverage between the conservative *Fox News* and the liberal *MSNBC* no longer held any credence (not that it ever had). They were forced to acknowledge the truth that had been presented to them all along, namely that the vast majority of mainstream U.S. Media was biased towards the Clinton camp in particular and the Democrats in general. After a brief discussion explaining to the *Maison de la Radio France* that Republicans Overseas' members could not and would not attend an event where there was no equal and fair media coverage for their chosen candidate, it was agreed that *Fox News* would be streamed during election night for this one instance as an exception to the *Maison de la Radio France's* exclusive agreement with *CNN*.

Did they honor their agreement on November 8th? Yes. And no. Most attendees to the event arrived in the evening at between 6:30 and 9pm. Blasting from all of the numerous big screen TVs around the gigantic facility was *CNN*. My quip to a fellow American, a Democrat Abroad member, was that I had seen enough from the *Clinton News Network* and wanted to see coverage from *Fox News* to get a sense of the other perspective. You know, in order to fill out the picture and get a more truthful and accurate

15

assessment of the election results.

His response? **1.** What do you mean *Clinton News Network*? At which point I cited the Donna Brazile emails proving that she had provided the debate questions to her candidate (when she was also the DNC Chairwoman at the very time as she was moderating the presidential candidate debate for *CNN*) prior to the debate. Cheater cheater. People have been expelled from university for less of an infringement of ethics and fair-play. His (the Democrat Abroad gentleman's) response? What leaked emails? Never heard a thing about that! And **2.** Well, you'll have to stay past midnight because they're not going to start streaming *Fox News* until after midnight.

Like most working-class people who live in Paris, I had to leave the event by midnight in order to catch the last métro home so I could get up and get to work the next day.

Once back home that night, I opened up a good dozen+ tabs on my computer and tracked the election results in the most efficient way I knew how: by watching the internet sites and twitter feeds of *Fox News, MSNBC, LA Times, CNN, Breitbart, Wa Post, NYT, RealDonaldTrump, KellyAnn Conway, HillaryClinton, Newsmax, RNC, DNC* and *AP*. Finally, hours later at just shy of 8:30 a.m. the *AP* called the election: Donald Trump is our newly elected 45th President of the United States.

How a Putin Fan Overseas Pushed Pro-Trump Propaganda to Americans, by Mike McIntire, *The New York Times*, December 17, 2016
Source: http://www.nytimes.com/2016/12/17/world/europe/russia-propaganda-elections.html

"Simple truth is that after 40 years of the right having no voice because the media was owned by the enemy, we were FORCED to become incredibly good at alternative media in a way the left simply can't grasp or handle," Mr. Dowson said. "Bottom line is: BREXIT, TRUMP and much more to follow." (Mr. Dowson refers to James Dowson of the *Patriot News Agency,* which, like the *NY Times* International edition, is based in the UK)

...In the email interview, Mr. Dowson said he was not supported by Russia in any way, and he accused critics of trying to tar conservatives as dupes of Moscow. ... "I look on this rebirth of McCarthy-type anti-Russian hysteria by the LEFT as a hilarious reaction born out of the left's inability to realize THEY elected Trump, not me, not the Russians, not even the right," he said via email.

Quizzical look at campaign, from viewpoint of overseas readers, by Declan Walsh, *The New York Times* Int'l Edition November 9th, 2016 page 6

Q: This election has seen the death of impartial news media. Will we ever see it again? (question submitted by Jack Jameson, Sweden, ex-New Jersey

A: It is certainly true that the polarized atmosphere of the election has spilled into American news media. At the conservative Fox News, the television host Sean Hannity has openly declared for Mr. Trump and uncritically aired conspiracy theories. At CNN, the political analyst Donna Brazile shared questions for CNN-sponsored candidate events (presidential debates) with the Clinton campaign. (The network has severed its ties with Ms. Brazile, a Democratic strategist who has been the interim chairwoman of the Democratic National Committee.)

Early in the campaign, many news outlets, including *The New York Times*, faced criticism that they had failed to subject Mr. Trump's unorthodox candidacy to sufficient scrutiny. Yet in recent months, news outlets have aggressively held both candidates accountable.

The Times exposed Mr. Trump's tax records from 1995, showing nearly $1billion in losses that allowed him to legally avoid paying any federal income taxes for years.

The *Washington Post* published a tape of Mr. Trump's aggressive sexual comments about women. Revelations from leaked emails published by WikiLeaks continue to embarrass the Clinton campaign. A bigger problem, I think, is that a growing number of American voters are losing confidence in major mainstream news sources and turning instead to social media, like Facebook and Twitter. One result is an echo chamber of like-minded views. This can increase the sense of political polarization. That is the paradox of this election: Americans have never had more access to so much information about the candidates; the question is whether they believe any of it.

AUTHOR: This same Irish observer-journalist of our 2016 presidential election had this further to say:

A measure of America's fever, by Declan Walsh, page 6 *NY Times* Int'l Edition November 9th 2016

"Thanks to Mr. Trump, fringe ideas are now aired in the mainstream, prejudice masquerading as fact."

AUTHOR: As the Paris-based travel correspondent for *USA Today*, and a minority American-expat Trump supporter here in the French capital, I was, in all honesty, struck aghast at my employer's stance on the election. For the first time in the history of the publication, they took a position against one of the presidential candidates.

After my initial reaction to this stance, that it now characterized the news media (my employer) as a tool of propaganda rather than an unbiased, non-partisan news source, I have continued to ponder just what would have, what could have, motivated an entire editorial board to take such a strong stance against the Republican candidate?

In my estimation the clue lies in the fact that the candidate they were staunchly, and now staunchly vocal, against was the candidate of the opposing party to the seated President. Eight years of Obama's administration as the crowned Pharaoh of the Democratic Party and by the end of those eight years most people left in any positions of power within our social and professional frameworks were, by definition, Obama adherents and Democrat sympathizers.

Does this mean that the powerful media elite were taking orders from an authority they perceived was

17

above them? Not necessarily. The coercion is much more insidious than that. It's commonly called co-optation. Meaning that 8 years of an autocratic-leaning seated ruler of the Democratic Party had resulted in a quelling of the cacophony of American voices where all that was left, especially when referring to people in high places, were those that agreed with the mindset as dictated by the prevailing power structure as set forth by the White House, our Executive Branch of government.

In other words, the only survivors left standing after 8 years of weeding out by an autocratic Democrat president and his minions were those who had chosen to "get on the right track," as that administration was so fond of saying. Of course "getting on the right track," was simply a euphemism used to express the notion that "they either think as we do or they're done; My way or the highway." Diversity of thought and differing of opinions no longer had any place in U.S. society. And this couldn't be more true the higher you climbed in the echelons of corporate media and politics.

Trump is Unfit For Presidency, *USA Today* Editorial Board, Sept 30 2016
Source: http://www.usatoday.com/story/opinion/2016/09/29/dont-vote-for-donald-trump-editorial-board-editorials-debates/91295020/

In the 34-year history of *USA TODAY*, the Editorial Board has never taken sides in the presidential race. Instead, we've expressed opinions about the major issues and haven't presumed to tell our readers, who have a variety of priorities and values, which choice is best for them. Because every presidential race is different, we revisit our no-endorsement policy every four years. We've never seen reason to alter our approach. Until now.

This year, the choice isn't between two capable major party nominees who happen to have significant ideological differences. This year, one of the candidates — Republican nominee Donald Trump — is, by unanimous consensus of the Editorial Board, unfit for the presidency.

Vote, But Not For Trump: Our View, *USA Today,* November 7, 2016
Source: http://www.usatoday.com/story/opinion/2016/11/07/donald-trump-hillary-clinton-election-day-editorials-debates/93449852/

Election Day has arrived (finally!), and polls suggest that an unusually high number of likely voters — 13% by one estimate — are undecided about the presidential race or are supporting minor-party candidates.

If you are one of them, we're guessing you're not uncommitted because you think you have so many good options.

You might see Donald Trump as a vehicle for shaking up Washington, but you're repelled by his narcissism, sexism and appeals to racism.

You might be impressed by Hillary Clinton's deep knowledge and experience, but you have concerns about her lack of candor, money-grubbing and careless (though, according to the FBI director, not criminal) handling of classified information.

You might have considered Libertarian Party nominee Gary Johnson, but you've been put off by his cluelessness on foreign affairs and periodic flakiness. You might think all the choices are flawed. And, like all human beings, they are. But are they equally flawed? No, not by a long shot.

As the Editorial Board said at the end of September, Trump's faults — his erratic temperament, ignorance and dishonesty — are so far outside the standard bounds of presidential politics as to be disqualifying.

AUTHOR: The next question I asked myself, then, was: From where does this influence come? Influence peddling comes in several forms – promises of power, promises of continued employment, as an alternative to personal and professional annihilation, and so forth. But how could this kind of influence have such far-reaching tentacles? In other words, the question I asked myself was if the White House isn't at the root of this influencing and indoctrination insofar as our media outlets are concerned, then who is?

Since I am a veteran-journalist of the early years of *The Huffington Post*, I thought I would start with the man rumored to have funded – and funded in a very big way – the creation of that blog-turned-national-media-platform, George Soros, billionaire at-large. Knowing as I did that Ms. Huffington was funded with tens of millions of dollars to start her blog after her failed California gubernatorial run in 2003 (Schwarzenegger, a Republican, won), I thought that this could be a good starting point. That the *Huffington Post* became the bully pulpit of then-presidential candidate Obama and his DNC-machine supporters by as early as 2007, I figured I was onto something. This is what I found:

Media Research Center, **Soros-Funded Lefty Media Reach More Than 300 Million Every Month**
Source: https://www.mrc.org/commentary/soros-funded-lefty-media-reach-more-300-million-every-month
MRC – "America's Media Watchdog"

"In fact, Soros funds nearly every major left-wing media source in the United States."

Laughably, Soros denies he has a media empire, despite spending easily more than $48 million on that empire and having top journalists from more than 30 major news organizations serving on the boards of groups he funds. "Another trick is to accuse your opponent of the behavior of which you are guilty, like Fox News accusing me of being the puppet master of a media empire," wrote Soros in the introduction to his new self-promotional book "The Philanthropy of George Soros." That book, appropriately, was written by former *New York Times* reporter Chuck Sudetic who now works for Soros' Open Society Foundations. It is the second such Soros promotional books written by a Times staffer. ...

Books, newspapers, radio stations, TV stations, websites and cutting edge videos. The pieces of the George Soros media empire are as diverse as the nations of the world and just as widespread. From nakedly partisan left-wing media like Think Progress, the blog for the Center for American Progress, and a TV show on MSNBC, to the supposedly impartial National Public Radio, Soros has impact on the flow of information worldwide.

It gives him incredible influence. Every month, reporters, writers and bloggers at the many outlets he funds easily reach more than 330 million people around the globe. The U.S. Census estimates the population of the entire United States to be just less than 310 million.

That's roughly the entire population of the United States with the population of Australia thrown in for good measure - every single month.

This information is part of an upcoming report by the Media Research Center's Business & Media Institute which has been looking into George Soros and his influence on the media.

Just counting 13 prominent operations of the 180 media organizations he has funded equals 332 million people each month. Included in that total are big players like NPR, which received $1.8 million from Soros, as well as the little known Project Syndicate and Public News Service, both of which also claim to reach millions of readers.

And that's really just the beginning. That tally takes into account only a few of the bigger Soros-funded media operations. Many numbers simply aren't available."Democracy Now!" - "a daily TV/radio news program, hosted by Amy Goodman and Juan Gonzalez" - is known for its left-wing take on global news. Its vitriol ranges from attacks on Blackwater founder Erik Prince and supporters of Andrew Breitbart (whom it calls 'Electronic Brownshirts'), to claims the U.S. is opposed to Arab democracy. Just that one Soros-funded operation is heard "on over 900 stations, pioneering the largest community media collaboration in the United States." But it posts no formal audience numbers. Phone calls to "Democracy Now!" were not returned.

...Soros wildly understates his own impact. On April 8, House Democratic leader Nancy Pelosi headlined a Boston conference on "media reform." She was joined by four other congressmen, a senator, two FCC commissioners, a Nobel laureate and numerous liberal journalists.

The event was sponsored by a group called Free Press, which has received $1.4 million from Soros. Free Press has two major agenda items - undermining Internet freedom by pushing so-called "net neutrality," and advocating for government-funded media to the tune of $35 billion a year. Many of those attending or speaking were affiliated with Soros-funded operations.

Free Press is just one of the better funded Soros groups. They also include the Center for American Progress ($7.3 million), which operates the heavily staffed Think Progress blog. That blog "now has 30 writers and researchers," according to Politico. Other well-funded operations include the investigative reporting operations at the Center for Public Integrity ($3.7 million) and Center for Investigative Reporting ($1.1 million), as well as Media Matters ($1.1 million) and the Sundance Institute ($1 million).

That's not all. "Soros' foundations gave 34 grants from 1997 to 2010 to local NPR member stations and specific programs that have totaled nearly $3.4-million, said the foundations' [spokesperson, Maria] Archuleta. Recipients included WNYC and Minnesota Public Radio," wrote outgoing NPR ombudsman Alicia Shepard.

In fact, Soros funds nearly every major left-wing media source in the United States....

The Soros 'echo chamber' is even larger. Many of his organizations have a media component - from New Orleans, where he funds *The Lens,* to nations that were once part of the former Soviet Union.

But he doesn't have a media empire.

AUTHOR: Below is an excerpt from an article about the culture of propaganda in the United States today written from the perspective of a psychology/behavioral science analysis.

Propaganda in America 2016, by Yoav Litvin, *CounterPunch,* November 4, 2016
Source: http://www.counterpunch.org/2016/11/04/propaganda-in-america-2016/

...A useful way of assessing the legitimacy of a democratically-elected regime is to examine the extent to which it relies on propaganda to maintain control. It is clear that with growing injustice comes more dissent, which forces the state to either confront the roots of injustice or increase its propaganda to subdue the populace. The militarization of American police forces signifies an acknowledgment of the limitations of repression by propaganda and a shift by the state toward reliance on traditional violence for control.

Propaganda then and now

One infamous American propaganda campaign was red-baiting, which reached its zenith during the term of Senator Joseph McCarthy in the 1950s. Red-baiting served the American profit-driven capitalist state well, as any persons categorized as communists/socialists, i.e. advocates for worker rights, were silenced in one way or another.

It is no coincidence that Hillary Clinton's campaign has been recently ramping up the use of anti-Russian rhetoric, a close relative of red-baiting. This form of propaganda evokes visceral fear reactions in Americans, who share a collective memory of its disastrous effects on individuals and society during the cold war. Fear typically drives people to seek guidance and protection from a strong man/woman. Currently, it is meant to prepare Americans for the possibility of confrontation with Russia and to divert attention from the incriminating information that WikiLeaks is releasing about Hillary Clinton and her shady dealings.

Chapter 3

The US Top Media Players by Numbers and Stats

The fault I find with most American newspapers is not the absence of dissent. It is the absence of news. With a dozen or so honorable exceptions, most American newspapers carry very little news. Their main concern is advertising.
                       – I.F. Stone, b.1907 d. 1989

USA Today, Wall Street Journal, New York Times are the top 3 U.S. Papers in circulation.

*Author's note: The following information is taken from the reported media's own websites, unless otherwise noted.

USA Today, based in McLean, Va. (just outside Wa. D.C.)

An innovator of news and information, we reflect the pulse of the nation and serve as the host of the American conversation — today, tomorrow and for decades to follow. We reach nearly three million readers daily, and our mobile applications attest to more than 22 million downloads on mobile devices. Gfk MRI Spring 2016 survey results report that *USA TODAY* has a daily readership of nearly 3 million. In June 2016, *USA TODAY* sites had nearly 88.3 million unique visitors and 870MM page views.

The New York Times

The Times has a daily print circulation of 590,000, and 1.1 million on Sunday.
As of the 1st quarter of 2016 the company counts close to 1.4 million digital-only subscriptions.
2014 New York Times' total circulation was 2.2 million with print circulation of 680,905, or 32% of the total.

WSJ
The Wall Street Journal reported a total average circulation of 2.3 million. The print edition comprised 1.4 million, or 59% of the total.
Source: http://www.wsj.com/articles/SB10001424052702304178104579535822452265610

Gannett Co.'s *USA Today* remained the top U.S. newspaper by total average daily circulation, which includes digital readers, while News Corp's *The Wall Street Journal* continued to have the largest print circulation, according to a data tracker Thursday.

TV Dominant News Networks

CNN, MSNBC, Fox News
http://www.journalism.org/2016/06/15/cable-news-fact-sheet/

Driven in part by interest in the 2016 presidential campaign, viewership increased for cable news channels in 2015.
In prime time – the premier time slot for advertisers – combined average viewership rose for the three major news channels (CNN, Fox News and MSNBC) by 8% to 3.1 million, according to Pew Research Center analysis of Nielsen Media Research data. The cable viewership increase was largely due to CNN, which experienced an especially sharp uptick, growing its evening viewership 38% to an average of 712,000 viewers. Cable-hosted presidential candidate debates helped drive some of the surge in viewership. Fox remained the evening viewership leader with 1.8 million (up 3% over 2014 levels). MSNBC was down 1% to 579,000.

Other News Sources – Both Conservative and Liberal

Breitbart
Total views for October 2016 on Breitbart.com was 85.8 million (indicating an 18% increase from the previous month)
https://www.similarweb.com/website/breitbart.com#overview

Investor's Business Daily
Source: http://myibd.investors.com/about-ibd/media-kit

Total Readership:

Monday/Weekly Edition Circulation   109,634

Source: Alliance for Audited Media - Quarterly Data Report Q4 2015

Investors.com

General Traffic Overview	Monthly
Total Page Views	33,865,147
Total Visits	10,053,441
Monthly Unique Visitors	6,085,352

Los Angeles Times
Sunday readership: 2.4 million Sunday circulation: 955,319 latimes.com: 32MM monthly UVs (online & mobile) Weekday readership: 1.5 million Weekday circulation: 690,870 latimes.com: 137MM monthly PVs (online & mobile)

Washington Post
Source: http://www.capitolcommunicator.com/washington-post-circulation-drops-37-percent-since-2009-states-dcrtv/
It showed the current average daily, Monday through Sunday, paid print circulation during the past year to be 395,234. That's down about 37% since 2009, when the paper's average daily circulation was 633,100."

However, while circulation of the print version has dropped, *The Post* website is regularly exceeding 50 million unique monthly visitors in the U.S. and crossed the 20 million point with international readers earlier this year. The August (2015) comScore numbers showed *The Washington Post*, with nearly 600 million page views and, in the past two weeks, The Post announced significant partnerships with Facebook. As of May 2013, its average weekday circulation was 474,767, according to the Audit Bureau of Circulations, making it the seventh largest newspaper in the country by circulation, behind *USA Today*, *The Wall Street Journal*, *The New York Times*, the *Los Angeles Times*, the *Daily News*, and the *New York Post*.

The Atlantic Monthly est. 1857
The number of paid subscribers today is roughly 486,000 as of December 2014 with 1.5 million readers; 21million digital unique viewers; newsstand sales average more than 50,000 copies a month. All told, they estimate at least 1.5 million people put their hands on each issue of *The Atlantic Monthly*. (*The Atlantic saw the highest increase in circulation, expanding slightly by 2% in 2015)
Source: http://rethink.theatlantic.com/static/img/upload/pdfs/TheAtlanticMediaKit_2015.pdf
Source: https://www.theatlantic.com/past/docs/about/atlhistf.htm
(*Source: http://www.journalism.org/2016/06/15/news-magazines-fact-sheet/)

The Huffington Post, Buzzfeed, Vice Media
As of October 2015
http://www.ibtimes.com/huffington-posts-us-traffic-tanks-2015-buzzfeed-vice-media-grow-2142607

The Huffington Post has seen a major decline in its monthly traffic coming from within the U.S. over the past year, while competitors such as *BuzzFeed* and *Vice Media* continue to grow, according to data provided by comScore to *International Business Times*. In September of last year, *HuffPost* pulled in around 113 million unique visitors and hit 126 million last November, but then steadily bled visitors into 2015 and throughout the year. Last month, it was down to 86 million.

As the No. 1 social publisher on Facebook,
we've learned these are the stories our readers
are most interested in reading and sharing."
– *Huffington Post*

Meanwhile, its biggest rivals in digital media, from *BuzzFeed* to *Vice* to *Business Insider*, have all seen growth over the same period. According to comScore, *Business Insider* rose from around 30 million to 41 million, while *Vice Media* blew up from around 10 million to 23 million.

BuzzFeed fluctuated from month to month but has continued to grow steadily, hitting 68 million in August 2014 and 85 million a year later

Newsmax Media – online, magazine, TV
Source: http://www.newsmax.com

Each month we reach over 14 million Americans who are affluent, well-informed and response-oriented adults

Newsmax has one of the highest concentrations of Baby Boomer consumers on the web.

•To 42 million U.S homes - Newsmax TV.

NPR - October 2016
Source: Npr.org
NPR is up 43%.
total weekly listeners for all NPR stations are about 36.6 million; weekly listeners for NPR Programming and Newscasts account for about 28.8 million of that total.
NPR's combined podcasts had 63 million unique downloads,
Use of the digital content available at NPR.org also climbed to record highs, reaching 40 million unique visitors in September for an average of over 36 million per month.

Democracy Now
Broadcast on the internet and by nearly 1,400 radio and television stations worldwide
it posts no formal audience numbers.
Source: Media Research Center https://www.mrc.org/commentary/soros-funded-lefty-media-reach-more-300-million-every-month

Rush Limbaugh
Source: http://www.gossipextra.com/2016/05/26/rush-limbaugh-audience-soaring-revenues-down-5997/
May 2016
While Limbaugh's audience hovers around 13 million listeners a week, a huge number at the age of fragmented audience and satellite radio, his advertisers are so scarce that some stations nationwide are losing money on their broadcasts of Limbaugh's show, according to Politico.

Influence, in Limbaugh's case, isn't necessarily translating into cold, hard cash:

In recent years, however, some of his most powerful long-time big city stations dropped the beachfront dweller, including *WABC* in New York City, as well as stations in Boston and Los Angeles.

And from *Politico* May 2016   http://www.politico.com/magazine/story/2016/05/is-rush-limbaugh-in-trouble-talk-radio-213914

(Limbaugh) who boasts some 600 affiliates on his self-styled "Excellence in Broadcasting [EIB] Network," and an estimated 13 million listeners per week. *The Rush Limbaugh Show* is easily the most-listened to talk radio program in the country. Mainstream media outlets from the *New York Times* to POLITICO have taken to frequently reporting its host's utterances as news. Limbaugh has also been credited with—or blamed for—the most startling political event of the season: Donald Trump's rise. (It's not that he endorsed Trump during the primaries; he just didn't go to war with him, as fellow radio right-wingers Mark Levin and Glenn Beck did.)

In recent years, Limbaugh has been dropped by several of his long-time affiliates, including some very powerful ones: He's gone from *WABC* in New York, *WRKO* in Boston and *KFI* in Los Angeles, for example, and has in many cases been moved onto smaller stations with much weaker signals that cover smaller areas.

Independent Journal Review
IJR.com
"most shared channel on social channels on election night 2016"
November 2016   26.1 million unique visitors
November 2015   21.5 million unique visitors
Established 2011
According to Alex Skatell, CEO, the site appeals to "independent minded" and "freedom-loving" people mainly in the midwest, in other words, outside of the biggest population centers.

Drudge Report
drudgereport.com
Users per month: 10.6 million
People per day: October 2016 3.7 million; January 2017 1.7 million

Univision
Source: Pew Research Center http://www.journalism.org/2016/06/15/hispanic-media-fact-sheet/

As of 2014, there are 55 million Hispanics in the U.S., making up 17% of the total population.

Univision, launched in 1962, currently has the largest audience of any Hispanic-oriented TV news network in the U.S.

Following a peak of about 2 million viewers in 2013, the average audience for Univision's flagship news program *Noticiero Univision* was down 2% to **1.86 million viewers in 2015**

Annual total revenue hovers at about just under $3B

(in 2014, including the closing of both <u>NBCLatino.com</u> and CNN Latino. Also, *Fusion* – a cable network owned by Univision – shifted its target audience from Hispanics to Millennials)

Telemundo
Nightly news program *Noticiero Telemundo* at about **850K nightly viewers**

Chapter 4

Everything - What The Media Got Wrong About Trump's Appeal To His Electorate

Chapter title taken from podcast interview on *Digiday* with Michael Wolff.
Source: http://digiday.com/publishers/digiday-podcast-michael-wolff-donald-trump/

A defiant victor tells leading TV figures they got it all wrong, by Michael M. Grynbaum and Sydney Ember, *New York Times* International Edition, November 23rd 2016
(re-printed from digital version November 21, 2016)
Source: http://www.nytimes.com/2016/11/21/business/media/trump-summons-tv-figures-for-private-meeting-and-lets-them-have-it.html?_r=0

"It had all the trappings of a high-level rapprochement: President-elect Donald J. Trump, now the nation's press critic in chief, inviting the leading anchors and executives of television news to join him on Monday for a private meeting of minds.

On-air stars like Lester Holt, Charlie Rose, George Stephanopoulos and Wolf Blitzer headed to Trump Tower for the off-the-record gathering, typically the kind of event where journalists and politicians clear the air after a hard-fought campaign.

Instead, the president-elect delivered a defiant message: You got it all wrong."

AUTHOR: Can you blame him? Never in the history of a U.S. Presidential election did the corporate media icons draw their wagons together in a circle in order to try to prevent one party's candidate from getting elected.

That issues went unreported, that the candidates' stances on key crises that our country is facing, such as infrastructure, went largely ignored in favor of the daily dish of dirt, can be blamed squarely on the media for not keeping its focus on what truly mattered.

But most importantly, that the elite liberal media not just ignored the desperate concerns of half the country's citizens, but even went so far as to deny that concerns existed nor had any merit, has deeper implications than that they simply "missed the boat," during this presidential election cycle.

A measure of America's fever, by Declan Walsh, *New York Times,* Int'l Edition, November 9th, 2016 (front page)

"To see Mr. Trump speak live is to understand his wild popularity with a section of the electorate. In three nationally televised debates, he often came across as a blustering, barracking bumbler. But in the gilded ballroom of the Venetian hotel and casino, he is in complete control.

He channels the energy of the crowd, listening as he speaks. When he hears the right note of approval, Mr. Trump amplifies is message and bounces it back, usually with one of his trademark three-word catchphrases. 'Drain the swamp!' the crowd yells on cue – a reference to the swamp upon which Washington was built."

AUTHOR: Michael Wolff writes for *The Hollywood Reporter* and is a former executive editor at *AdWeek*. He scored the first interview with Steve Bannon, after President Trump announced his appointment as his strategic adviser. Steve Bannon was formerly the CEO of Breitbart News before being tapped by President Trump to run his election campaign alongside Reince Priebus. And now to be his Chief Strategist in the White House.

They are 'taking the bait': Columnist Michael Wolff on why the media blew it on Trump, *by Brian Morrissey, Digiday,* November 23, 2016
Source: http://digiday.com/publishers/digiday-podcast-michael-wolff-donald-trump/

Michael Wolff – podcast interview on Digiday
"Literally everything. I can't think of another instance in which the media was so off in its predictions, its evaluations, in the ways in which it hedged its bets. Every person and every outlet, and I mean this across the board - networks, cable stations, newspapers - the fundamental assumption was not only was Donald Trump unfit to be president but that he could never be president, would never be president. If the American people didn't stop him from being president, the media would stop him with their opprobrium and their collective decision he couldn't be." - Michael Wolff

Interview Question: Brian Morrissey from Digiday Podcast
Does this say more about the media now? Because this was a widely held stance in elite institutions across the board by elite I mean we were being told by David Plouff and all these apparent political geniuses that this is simply not going to happen. Is it the media's fault for missing this? Or is it not really the media's fault?

Answer: Michael Wolff
It is the media's fault. At the end of the day if an event happens which catches you, the media... I mean A. It's our job to get things right and to be accurate. And B. to at least provide for the possibility that untoward and unexpected things can happen... And in an election where the choice is binary, it seems pretty reasonable that you would at least have a scenario in your back pocket in which the other guy might win. And that was totally absent. Absent to such an extent that in that moment when he won, in that hour where the shift on election night was clear essentially the media, everyone, was in tears...

Michael Wolff - Cont'd
....Media's failing at the basics

"I think what's required is for the media to do its job. I feel deeply the media hasn't done its job. It's abdicated its responsibility, has lost itself somewhere. Right now it's an interesting moment in which the media looks at Donald Trump as a threat instead of a story, possibly the biggest story of our time maybe the most interesting story. Certainly a story that needs to be told in rather conventional ways. Who are these people, what do they want, what motivates them, where are they from, where are they going — just basic storytelling.

"I thought these people have won an election, so now is the time to go in and say who are you and what do you think. We are not in an oppositional moment right now; that has passed. I actually asked very few questions. I said tell me who you are. He talked and I took notes. Yes, you do want to be stenographers. That's a very significant piece of journalism. We don't want to hear [the reporter]. Write it down. You're there to literally convey what someone in power says, and you bring it to people who want to know. Journalism is now a profession filled with people who are not journalists. They're all under 25, talking to people under the age of 25. Let me send the message: stenographer is what you're supposed to be.

Comment Thread on this Digiday Podcast :
Tuatha DeDanaan

I've never met a liberal who doesn't spew his/her opinions at anyone who will listen: they love to lecture, they love to "share", while we conservatives sit back, nod politely, and wait for them to finish with the emotionally-driven and fashionable opinions *de jour* that pepper every conversation.

Conversely, I've never met a conservative who vaults over cube walls to shout down a liberal, or who protests and sulks like a 4th grader when his/her candidate loses.

This is why the polls are so skewed: conservatives aren't participating. They keep their own counsel, but they vote. In droves.

And the media is blind to them, because libs are parading around shouting their opinions at anyone who will listen, drowning out competing voices. But in the voting booth, their opinions have no more weight than those of any other citizen.

Trump v the media: did his tactics mortally would the fourth estate?, by Ed Pilkington, *The Guardian*, November 22nd 2016
Source: https://www.theguardian.com/media/2016/nov/22/election-2016-donald-trump-media-coverage?

((Author paraphrase in parantheses)Many media pundits assumed that the *WaPost* leaked Billy Bush interview from over a decade earlier would)"... hand female voters, and thus the presidency, to Clinton. They didn't – 53% of white women voted for Trump, according to exit polls.

Jorge Ramos, the lead news anchor at Univision, predicted on election day that Trump would lose because he had turned his back on the Spanish-language media. Didn't happen – almost one in three Hispanics backed him, to Ramos's bafflement."

... But BuzzFeed's Ben Smith makes the point that, important though such post-election soul-searching is, it should not obscure the fact that there was plenty of hard-hitting reporting done even early on. "The *Washingon Post, New York Times*, we at *BuzzFeed, Politico*, the *Guardian* and many more, gave a thoroughly detailed account of him. Anyone who was surprised by the person who emerged during the campaign really wasn't paying attention."

Media warily hoping for change in Trump, by Jim Rutenberg, *New York Times* International Edition, November 15, 2016 page 9

...For their part, American newsrooms are conducting their own reassessments, vowing to do a better job covering the issues that animated his supporters and acknowledging that Mr. Trump tapped into something in the national mood, the power of which they failed to grasp...
The wrong lesson to take from the past year is that reporters should let up in their mission of reporting the truth, wherever it leads...

But if there is one thing we learned this year, it was the wisdom of the old mnemonic device for the spelling of 'assume' (makes an 'ass' out of 'u' and 'me').

AUTHOR: "We Were Blindsided" -The unanimous cry of the liberal US media echo chamber.

Read a catalogue of commentaries by various members of the media who covered the 2016 U.S. Presidential election in the following sources. An example commentary, by Moss of *New York Magazine*, was taken from *The Guardian* article (source 1 noted below) which draws from a lengthy compilation assembled by the *Columbia Journalism Review* (source 2 noted below).

Source 1:https://www.theguardian.com/us-news/2016/nov/22/journalists-media-election-2016-donald-trump
Source 2: http://www.cjr.org/special_report/trump_media_press_journalists.php

Adam Moss, editor-in-chief, *New York Magazine*: The one thing that I think even quality media did terribly wrong in this election was that they – and I put us in the same boat – didn't force a focus on actual content.

The absence of conversation about climate change, and the fact that we have absolutely no idea today what Donald Trump actually truly wants to do about anything, is a catastrophic error on the media's part, and lots of other people's part.

Covering Trump: An Oral History of An Unforgettable Campaign, *Columbia Journalism Review* (cited in above Guardian article), November 22, 2016
Source: http://www.cjr.org/special_report/trump_media_press_journalists.php

AUTHOR: In my commentary above I noted that the assessment that the U.S. Liberal mainstream media "got it all wrong" has deeper implications than just "missing the boat" or being "out to lunch."

There are two primary scenarios one can draw from the fact that all the way up until the wee hours of election night, November 8th 2016, the corporate media were telling the public that the Democratic candidate (Hillary Clinton) had the presidency in the bag:

The first is that the media doing the reporting, the 25-and-under-year-olds that Mr. Wolff alludes to in his interview cited above, simply didn't listen to what Trump's supporters had to say. Their job is to be present at the political rallies and to speak with members of the candidates' election campaign as well as supporters at as many events they can humanly attend while on assignment. To comprehend Mr. Walsh's insightful commentary in his *NYT* report of his firsthand experience attending a Trump rally, the fever pitch of support that President Trump was able to raise in his supporters left an indelible knowing that he was and is speaking straight to the heart of his electorate. And that his supporters supported him passionately and that his comprehension and command of their concerns for the future of America gave him the edge over the other candidate for having his finger on the pulse of this vast segment of the American people.

Since it's reasonable to assess that this wasn't an isolated incident – the one described in the above-cited article by Mr. Walsh - but was a phenomenon endemic to most of President Trump's rallies, what were all the other reporters doing? The only two possible answers is that they were either A.) not attending Trump rallies so they had no firsthand, direct experience of the resonance the Republican candidate had with his supporters or, B.) The were attending the rallies and choosing to ignore what it was they were seeing with their own eyes.

Either answer is not just unsatisfactory but deeply dismaying.

The second scenario to draw as a cause for the mainstream media missing the boat in the 2016 U.S. Presidential election is that they were purposefully intending to paint a picture to their viewers/ listeners/ readers. This picture, frighteningly, adhered more to their employers' and editorial boards' consensus – a sort of #NeverTrump platform to put it succinctly – than the reality they were witnessing. To take this line of reasoning further, these reporters were not witnessing, listening to and documenting this Trump phenomenon, one that can justly be defined as a modern-day American revolution, but were fabricating a reality and bending perceptions to adhere to the seated power structure's intended and wished-for outcome.

And whereas the first scenario is deeply worrisome, the second scenario is downright frightening.

Chapter 5

How Can Data-Centric Reporting Get The Data Wrong?

The 2016 U.S. Presidential election was designed to be different from any other prior elections in the United States. This election, we were told, was going to rely heavily on data reporting. Everyone "knows" that "numbers don't lie." So in an attempt to obfuscate the mainstream liberal media's propensity to manipulate facts in order to tell their preferred story, reporting was to heavily rely upon data.

The picture that emerged by the end of the election cycle, however, was that data can be manipulated and was manipulated. And while numbers may not lie, the sources from which those numbers are culled can and often do fudge the facts.

Polls became a daily tally, even a daily war cry, by both presidential candidates' camps leading up to the November 8th election. The entire cartel of mainstream media outlets were unified throughout the campaign in releasing poll numbers that had Hillary ahead of Trump. All, with the exception of one – the *LA Times*/ USC poll which consistently placed Trump ahead by a few points. There was one other source that was also accurately tallying the polls and that was *Investors Business Daily. B*ut since that media is more of a niche media, I am sticking with the story line that all the major corporate U.S. Mainstream media outlets, save for one – the *LA Times* - misrepresented data reporting and presented skewed polling numbers throughout the presidential campaign, all the way up until Trump won the electoral college vote in a landslide on the morning of November 9th, 2016.

Since the daily polling tallies became as much of an anchor of election reporting as did Trump's Tweets, it is essential that we examine more closely just how these numbers were allowed to be so skewed. Again, it's essential that we ask, Was this human error and simple oversight, or was there intention behind the obfuscation of the story the true data and facts were revealing?

How did pollsters get election so wrong? By Nathan Bomey, *USA Today* November 10th 2016, News 3a

"In the final average 4-way polls tracked by RealClearPolitics, Clinton led 45.5% to Trump's 42.2%, Libertarian Gary Johnson's 4.7% and Green Party candidate Jill Stein's 1.9%. Polls that consistently gave Clitnon a comfortable lead in recent weeks included *Bloomberg Politics*, *CBS News*, *Fox News*, *Reuters*/Ipsos, *USA Today*/Suffolk, Quinnipiac, Monmouth, *Economist*/*YouGov*, and *NBC News*/SM, according to RealClearPolitics.

Of 67 national polls tracking a 4-way race since the start of October (2016), only four gave Trump the lead, according to RealClearPolitics. Of 61 national polls tracking a 2-way race during that period, six gave Trump the lead.

And all six were the *L.A. Times*/USC poll.

… One assessment, the Princeton Election Consortium, raised eyebrows with its projection that Clinton had a 99% chance of prevailing.

AUTHOR: As noted above, another polling source that conservatives were looking to in the final weeks before the election was the *Investor's Business Daily* news.

Trump Lead Widens To 2, His Biggest Yet, Despite 'November Surprise': *IBD/TIPP* Poll
Source: http://www.investors.com/politics/trump-lead-widens-to-2-his-biggest-yet-despite-november-surprise-ibdtipp-poll/

IBD/TIPP presidential election tracking poll

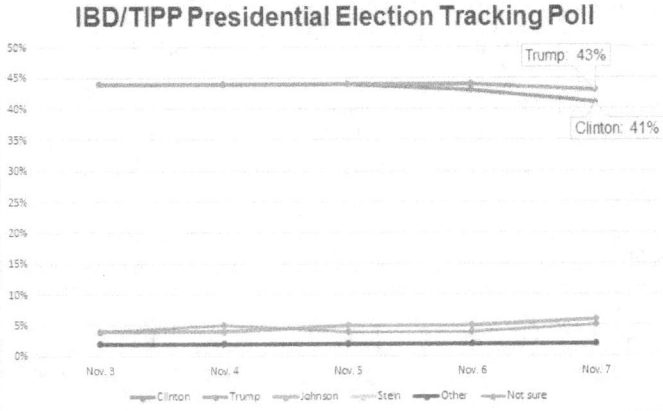

The unrounded poll numbers give Trump a 2.4 percentage point advantage over Clinton in the four-way race, 43.1% to 40.7%. Trump and Clinton had essentially been deadlocked for four days through Friday, but Trump moved into the lead Saturday

Source:IBD/TIPP presidential election tracking poll breakdown http://www.investors.com/politics/ibd-tipp-presidential-election-poll/

With one day to go, Donald Trump extended his lead over Hillary Clinton, 43% to 41%, according to the latest IBD/TIPP presidential tracking poll. That comes after a third bombshell from FBI Director James Comey, who announced Sunday he would not indict Clinton for her email scandal.
Trump's two-point lead now matches his largest so far during the 20 days of polling.
Libertarian candidate Gary Johnson gets 6% of the vote, Green Party candidate Jill Stein just 2%.
In a two-way matchup that excludes the two third-party candidates, however, Clinton still holds a 43% to 42% lead over Trump, with 9% of those responding saying they were "unsure" for whom they would vote.

For more analysis of the IBD/TIPP poll:
Results based on survey of 1107 likely voters conducted from 11/4 - 11/7. Margin of error: +/- 3.1 percentage points.

The IBD/TIPP poll — a collaboration between Investor's Business Daily (IBD) and TechnoMetrica Market Intelligence (TIPP) — has been the most accurate poll in recent presidential elections.

The latest results for the IBD/TIPP Presidential Election Tracking Poll will be released each morning by 6 a.m. ET.

Also look for daily videos with analysis of the latest results on our Facebook page and on Investors.com. About IBD/TIPP Poll

Final IBD/TIPP Poll Results

Trump Holds 2-Point Lead Over Clinton As Election Day Arrives: IBD/TIPP Poll

AUTHOR: See more Polling Graphs: The polling data you'll find here http://www.investors.com/politics/ibd-tipp-presidential-election-poll/ includes category breakdowns by region, age, income, race, education, party, ideology, parental status, gender, religion, household description and more.

It's interesting to hear other journalists weigh in on their assessment of the presidential candidate polls....

Accomplices or antagonists: how the media handled the Trump, by Ed Pilkington, *The Guardian*, November 22, 2016 https://www.theguardian.com/us-news/2016/nov/22/journalists-media-election-2016-donald-trump

Scott, the Associated Press: I think we all need to look at the role of horse-race polling. Is the story of the day really who's up and who's down in the latest poll? Or would we be better off spending more time talking with voters, trying to learn a little bit more about what they're thinking? The only poll that matters is the one that's taken on election day.

How did pollsters get election so wrong? By Nathan Bomey *USA Today* International Edition November 10th 2016, News 3a

"Pollsters flubbed the 2016 presidential election in seismic fashion.

Donald Trump's strong performance dealt a crushing blow to the credibility of the nation's pollsters, calling into question their mathematical models, assumptions and survey methods.

Several months of polls pegged Hillary Clinton as the leader in the polarizing race and as the leader in many key battleground states.

But Trump's surge crushed the conventional wisdom among pollsters. Late Tuesday, it appeared he was far outpacing projections across the board.

...the results suggest pollsters may have wildly underestimated the number of hidden Trump voters – people who stampeded to the ballot box on Election Day but never showed up on the radar of suveyors.

One notable exception among pollsters: *The Los Angeles Times/* University of Southern California tracking poll consistently pegged Trump as the leader throughout the final months of the campaign – and to much derision from political pundits.

"Arie Kapteyn, director of the University of Southern California's (USC) Dornsrife Center for Economic and Social Research, which jointly runs the poll, said some voters were apparently sheepish about admitting to a human pollster that they were backing Trump. But the *L.A. Times/* USC poll was based on an internet survey of a recruited group of voters.

'There's some suggestion that Clinton supporters are more likely to say they're Clinton supporters than Trump supporters are to say they're a Trump supporter, Kapteyn said.

... " But Michael Traugott, professor at the University of Michigan's Center for Political Studies, said he doesn't believe the differences between internet-based polls and phone-based polls explains the whopping disparity. He estimated shortly before midnight (Nov. 8th 2016) that overall turnout would equal about 130 million voters, down from an expected 135 million. 'But if the lower turnout was disproportionately among Democrats, that obviously would have hurt Clinton,' Traugott said."

Oceans of data and few facts, by Sapna Maheshwari, *New York Times* International Edition, November 15, 2016. page 8

...When Mr. Trump won the election last week, an industry that prides itself on always knowing what motivates and excites the American public was in a state of shock. ...Advertisers, like many others, 'may have found ourselves in bubbles of our own making,' said Rishad Tobaccowala, chief strategist for the Publicis Groupe.

According to Sarah Hofstetter, chief exec of digital agency 360i, the disconnect between Mr. Trump's win and the predictions from polls and forecasters threw into question 'the rules of market research,' traditionally rooted in surveys, interviews and discussions with focus groups in controlled settings.

That information should now be supplemented with 'social listening,' on Twitter, Reddit and other parts of the internet and behavioral data including what people are searching for online.... It's a wake-up call, she said. 'One data set is not going to give you the full picture, because with people, what people say is not always what they think or what they do, whether intentional or not.'"...

Wendy Clark, the chief executive of DDB North America and a former Coca-Cola marketing executive, said the election showed 'facts are somewhat negotiable.' Ms. Clark spent some time working with Mrs. Clinton's campaign last year, a rumor confirmed last month when an email she wrote about the importance of Mrs. Clinton's logo was disclosed by WikiLeaks.

'Facts are sort of, I might take them or I might not," she said. 'They're certainly discretionary now, so there is that notion as a marketer and advertiser of understanding we live in a postfactual democracy."

...Some see a broader lesson in the rejection of experience by the electorate. Richard Edelman, the chief executive of the public relations company, Edelman, said Mr. Trump's use of Twitter...showed the power of peer-to-peer communication.

'The more effective messaging might be from the mass population as opposed to using celebrities and using media and academics.'"

AUTHOR: WTF is a post-factual democracy? (pls. Refer to Glossary at the end of this book for a definition of 'post-factual'.)

This phrase "postfactual" or "post-truth" is another example of one of the catch-phrases, along with "echo chamber," "normalize" and "reality bubble" being bandied about post-election. The title of Jonathan Freedland's *The Guardian* article sums it up:

Don't call it post-truth. There's a simpler word: lies, by Jonathan Freedland, The Guardian, December 16, 2016
Source: https://www.theguardian.com/commentisfree/2016/dec/16/not-post truth-simpler-words-lies-aleppo-trump-mainstream

AUTHOR: It's telling to what degree advertisers and marketing executives are ready to offer their opinions as to why and how they so gravely mistook the concerns, needs and desires of the American public. In essence it is testament to the fact that large swaths of the American public were being ignored by not just the media but also by Advertising executives, usually based in huge metropolitan cities like

NYC and LA, hired by national brands to listen to and then speak to the American consumer-at-large. Obviously they didn't and they weren't.

Why Pollsters Got The Election So Wrong and What It Means for Marketers, by Jack Neff, *Ad Age,* November 10, 2016
Source: http://adage.com/article/campaign-trail/pollsters-wrong-means-marketers/306697/

...the shame belonged to Trump voters, many of them unwilling to admit, particularly to live human beings on the other end of the phone, their plans to vote for the president-elect.
That was an effect that Trafalgar Group, a small Atlanta-based Republican-affiliated polling firm, began noticing during the Republican primaries. So it developed a system to counteract the effect. Trafalgar started asking voters not only who they planned to vote for, but also who they thought their neighbors would vote for. The latter percentage consistently came out higher number than the former, said Robert Cahaly, senior strategist.

"On a live poll, the deviation was that Trump was understated probably 6%-7%, and on an automatic poll it was probably understated 3%-4%," Mr. Cahaly said. Using its adjusted numbers, Trafalgar predicted upsets for Mr. Trump in Pennsylvania and Michigan. And the firm's 306-232 prediction in the overall Electoral College vote may well end up matching the final total. The methodology got a "C" from Nate Silver's FiveThirtyEight.com, but it ended up being closer than FiveThirtyEight's system of consolidating results from a large number of polls that mostly were skewed wrongly toward Hillary Clinton.

... "Mr. Chadwick has been warning for years about the growing issues of survey research caused by ever more reluctant respondents, particularly in phone research, something that he believes may have helped hide some of that "silent" Trump vote but also causes growing issues for brand research.

'Particularly people who are feeling disenfranchised, angry, they're not going to pick up the phone for a poll, and even if they do may not want to tell a stranger who they're going to vote for,' Mr. Chadwick said. Simon Chadwick is the founding and managing partner of Cambiar, a consulting firm for market-research agencies and their investors.

....It's worth noting that some organizations that have tracked the presidential horse race in the past -- including Gallup and Pew, opted not to this year. Growing uncertainty about results may make such efforts more likely to cause embarrassment than showcase capabilities.

Women who helped Trump win, by Sheryl Gay Stolberg, *New York Times* International Edition, November 14, 2016 page 5

"Celinda Lake, a Democratic pollster, said the party had expected a 'surge of women' to support Mrs. Clinton, but that did not happen. While Mrs. Clinton did better with women in almost every demographic group, Ms. Make said, 'Trump won very solidly the white women's vote, and we know that was fed by white, blue-collar women.'

Ms. Biro comes close to fitting that mold; although she considers herself middle class, she did not go to college. And Nazareth, a middle-class community in Northampton County, is the kind of community where Trump did well. Yet sitting in the kitchen of her tidy Cape Cod-style home here, with the Trump-Pence signs will stuck in the front yard, Ms. Biro expressed the same hopes and fears for the country that many of Mrs. Clinton's supporters have.

'Hopefully he's going to try to unite people,' she said of the president-elect. 'We have to try to help people heal, so people can learn to trust, and have faith that things are going to be O.K.'"

Three Democratic Delusions, by Michael Medved, *USA Today* International Edition, December 1, 2016 page 10A

...First they (Democrats) seek comfort in Hillary Clinton's popular vote margin of more than two million,...This overview not only undermines Democrats' claims to majority party status, but argues against the notion that they can blame November's loss on an especially unpopular candidate.

In fact, Hillary Clinton's percentage of the popular vote (48%) was typical of other recent Democratic candidates like John Kerry in 2004 (48.3%), Al Gore in 2000 (48.4%) and even her husband, Bill Clinton, in his successful 1996 re-election bid (49.2%). Hillary actually won a much larger proportion of the electorate than Bill did in his first presidential win, where he commanded only 43% against George H. W. Bush and Ross Perot.

...Results nearly everywhere showed a Republican wave, not just a magical Donald Trump appeal. Republicans won at least 21 Senate seats to the Democrats' 12, cemented control of at least 33 governorships to the Democrats' 15, and captured at least 240 House seats to 194 for the opposition. These are crushing numbers and the GOP has now won House control four elections in a row...

The Donkey Party, in other words, faces a deeper dilemma than a single lackluster candidate. Members may try to reassure themselves with polls showing more Americans identifying as Democrats than Republicans, but they should remember that self-described "independents" tend to vote GOP in election after election, while the recent contest casts serious doubt on reliability of "scientific" polling.
....

How I missed the signs of a Trump win, by Bill Sternberg, *USA Today* Opinion, November 15, 2016 page 10A (*Note: Bill Sternberg is Editor of the Editorial Page of *USA Today*)

"How I missed the signs of a Trump win. The clues, there all along, should have made me question the polls.... North Canton, home to he massive brick factory where Hoover vacuum cleaners used to be manufactured. Hoover and later owners had shifted thousands of jobs to Texas, Mexico and ultimately China. The union hall across Main Street from the mostly vacant plant was about to close down for good....

When people back home in deep-blue Maryland asked how Trump could possibly have won the GOP

40

nomination, and whether he had a shot in November, I'd take out my smartphone and show them a photo of the former Hoover plant.

Sure enough, Trump's improbable path to victory sliced straight through the Rust Belt states of Pennsylvania, Ohio, Michigan and Wisconsin and their counties flush with white, working-class voters.

My final clue that an upset might be in the making came from a working-class Hispanic woman I know. A few days before Election Day, I asked her how she planned to vote. Considering Trump's denigration of Mexican immigrants and a Latina beauty queen, I presumed she'd be firmly and enthusiastically in the Clinton camp. But she said she was undecided, concerned that Clinton might end up in jail if elected. Her chauvinistic husband, she added, didn't think a woman should be president.

And sure enough, surveys of people after they voted suggested that Trump did far better than expected among Hispanics, about as well as Mitt Romney did in 2012. Anecdotal evidence?

Absolutely.

But after this year's unexpected outcome, who are you going to believe? Pollsters or your own eyes?

AUTHOR: Here is an email circulating since the election results and one that tries to explain the claims by Clinton's camp that she won the popular vote. It's an excellent example of how data-centric reporting can be manipulated to tell one story that can be seen as factually correct, yet is less than truthful and does not paint an accurate picture:

Trump - 62,972,226 electoral - 306

Clinton- 62,277,750 electoral - 232

Dear Fellow Americans,

We hear a cacophony of blaring and bleating from the media and the Hillary gaggle that she won the popular vote and therefore she should be president, 60,839,497 to 60,265,847. 47.8% to 47.3% with the remaining 4.9% going to the other candidates. But here are the facts:

Trump won the popular vote in 31 states to her 19 and DC 62% to her 19%. Trump led in the total popular vote for all states except California.

Hillary won California 5,860,714 to Trump's 3,151,821. 61.6% to 33.1% exclusive of the other candidates. Thus California gave Hillary the popular vote for all states as claimed by the Democrats and their media stooges. But deduct her California vote from her national vote leaving her with 54,978,783, and deduct Trump's California vote from his national total, leaving him with 57.113.976, he wins in a landslide in the other 49 states, 51.3% to her 48.7%.

So, in effect, Hillary was elected president of California and Trump was elected president of the rest of the country by a substantial margin.

This exemplifies the wisdom of the Electoral College, to prevent the vote of any one populace state from overriding the vote of the others. Trump's Campaign Manager, Kellyanne Conway, whose expertise is polling, saw this early on and devised her strategy of , "6 pathways to the White House." This meant ignoring California, with its huge Democrat majority, and going after the states that would give him the necessary Electoral votes to win, FL, NC, MI, PA, OH and WI.

One other tidbit:
California is one of 11 "welfare states" where there are more people living off the gov't dole than there are working for a living.

*AUTHOR: Note – there is a similar email circulating that states it is New York (not California) where the majority of Hillary votes were cast tipping the popular vote in her favor and that she qualifies therefore to be the president of New York.

AUTHOR:
In sum, the truth of human prejudice, that we see only what we want to see, held throughout the election season and was reinforced, rather than analytically and impartially busted apart, by corporate "mainstream" media outlets and trusted political "expert" pundits and pollsters.

So if even data-centric analysis and truth in numbers can be distorted to such a degree that they tell the story that the storyteller wants told, where do we stand then in regards to subjective judgments and topics that require analytical dissection?

It's telling, too, that the above-cited analysis of national polling sources from *USA Today* (Bomey, November 10th) omits the one other consistently accurate source, namely the IBD/TIPP poll. That poll has accurately predicted U.S. Presidential election results since 2004, dutifully earning its moniker: "TIPP is America's most accurate pollster, having come #1 in both the 2004 and 2008 Presidential elections." And now also the 2012 and 2016 elections. (http://www.tipponline.com/about-tipp)

Chapter 6

Was There An Agenda? What Was It? And Why?

Every time we are confronted with a new revolution, we take to the opium pipes
of our own propaganda. – I.F. Stone

"The natural response of the media is to suck up to power...most of the media are not contrarians, they
march in step." - Michael Wolff

They are "taking the bait": Columnist Michael Wolff on why the media blew it on Trump, by
Brian Morrissey, *Digiday Podcast*, November 23, 2016
Source: http://digiday.com/publishers/digiday-podcast-michael-wolff-donald-trump/

AUTHOR: The liberal mainstream media as the self-appointed electoral college. This is how to
accurately describe the politicized media landscape throughout the 2016 U.S. Presidential campaign.

Donald Trump – Addressing a crowd at a gala dinner "roast" during the 2016 campaign
https://www.youtube.com/watch?v=XVPDgmJZoPM
(starts at 8:02)
"And I got the chance to meet the people that are working so hard to get her (Hillary) elected – there
they are (pointing at the guests present at the gala dinner) – the heads of *NBC, CNN, CBS, ABC*. There's
the *NY Times* right over there and the *Washington Post*. " - Donald Trump

Unshackled Trump loses Republican support, *USA Today* International Edition, October 23, 2016
page 9A

And another headline on the same *USA Today* page: **Twitter tirade shows an unhinged candidate**

AUTHOR: The day the above headlines appeared in *USA Today*, I happened to be at a meeting with some of the members of Republicans Overseas in Paris. They had just come off an RNC conference call earlier that day on which Mr. Priebus had stated that the RNC was still 100% behind Trump. He had firmly stated on the call, I was told, that the Republicans still backed their candidate completely, including House Speaker Paul Ryan. When I showed them this headline, color immediately rose to their cheeks and the only words they could find to express their thoughts were that the headlines in *USA Today* were simply inaccurate.

Media Malpractice? Media Bias and The 2016 Election, by Tom Westervelt and Raghavan Mayur, *Investor's Business Daily*, Monday, 21 November 2016
Source: http://www.tipponline.com/news/election-2016/792-media-malpractice-media-bias-and-the-2016-election

After an election cycle that saw the news media so clearly bent on belittling and defeating a candidacy, media outlets must now conduct their own soul searching as they come to terms with an election result that caught them by surprise. ...

But (*NYT*'s Jim) Rutenberg's point about the news media overlooking the growing populist sentiment among Americans comes close to identifying what, in our opinion, is the root cause of the media's underestimation of Trump's support, and media bias in general. As many media outlets are headquartered in major cities, journalists and pundits are sheltered in the bubble of a shared elite liberal mentality.

Maybe if members of the elite media had stepped outside their comfort zone and investigated the problems facing the working class in the Midwest, they would not have been so wrong regarding the election.

AUTHOR: For the below excerpts from journalists involved in covering the historic 2016 presidential election, I turn once again to the *Columbia Journalism Review,* as re-published in *The Guardian.*

(this article – *The Guardian's* **Accomplices or antagonists: how the media handled the Trump phenomenon,** November 22, 2016 - source is taken from the Columbia Journalism Review reporting team **CJR's reporting team**: Shelley Hepworth, Vanessa Gezari, Kyle Pope, Carlett Spike, Cory Schouten, David Uberti and Pete Vernon)
Source: https://www.theguardian.com/us-news/2016/nov/22/journalists-media-election-2016-donald-trump

Rebecca Traister, writer, New York magazine: I think a lot of the press treated Hillary like she was going to be the president, and held her to account for that.

Molly Ball, politics writer, the Atlantic: You'd write stories saying both candidates are historically unpopular, but [people would] say, "Yes, but Trump is a bit more unpopular," or "Yes, but Trump is more of a liar," or "Yes, but Trump is more this or that." And sure, we should be noting in the pieces that there are differences of degree, but in a two-party system you're always going to be comparing the two candidates. A lot of liberals wanted us to portray a Hillary Clinton who didn't exist, a Hillary Clinton who was thronged by adoring fans. I covered Hillary Clinton. I never covered a candidate before where you would go to her own events and half the people there would say they didn't really like her.

Gerard Baker, editor, the Wall Street Journal: I'm really proud of the journalism we did. Other people were so focused on Trump's apparent flaws and questions about his own character that they simply looked past the bigger political phenomenon going on. Some reporters saw it as their role to stop this man from becoming president. They put themselves in the role of partisans. They were saying that if you voted for Trump, you were implicitly a racist. It's easier to write about someone and his character than it is to go out into the country and report.

Wallace, Fox News Sunday: The problem I have with the *Times,* and frankly a lot of other newspapers, is that at some point they decided that Trump was beyond the pale, and that he should not be treated as a legitimate presidential candidate. You're entitled to your opinion, I just don't think you're entitled to your opinion on the front page of the paper.

Moss, New York magazine: We don't pretend to objectivity, but we do, as a rule over the years, try to maintain some kind of even-handedness. We abandoned that because we felt the threat of his candidacy and presidency was too great.

Chris Wallace, host, Fox News Sunday: The reasons Fox succeeds are because there are millions of people out there – and sure O'Reilly is popular and Hannity is popular and Kelly is popular – but I don't think that is why Fox News succeeds. It's because people think that the mainstream media has a single focus, and there are multiple foci on what's important in the world.

Accomplices or antagonists: how the media handled the Trump phenomenon, *The Guardian,* by Ed Pilkington, November 22, 2016
Source: https://www.theguardian.com/media/2016/nov/22/election-2016-donald-trump-media-coverage?

"The Nieman Lab counted 360 titles that backed Clinton, including the *Dallas Morning News* which sided with a Democratic candidate for the first time since 1940, and *USA Today* which endorsed the first presidential candidate, period, in its 36-year history. By contrast, Trump drew a paltry 11 endorsements. Such overwhelming consensus from the nation's press – but was anybody listening?

　　...did the press go too far in abandoning its traditional even-handedness and unrestrainedly attacking Trump?...

Ginger Gibson, reporter, Reuters: You had candidates that got up and insulted you every day. They told everybody that you were liars, that you were making everything up. Those are the things that challenge you when you're at your desk and you're talking about stories with your co-workers. You have to sort of talk through and be like, "How do we know we're not dismissing something because the thing that got said is, *You're a liar and you make things up and you're trying to throw the election?*"

Deb, CBS News: I was at Trump HQ. As the night went on, you could sense that something is wrong here in terms of what we expected tonight. Not just reporters, but campaign staff. As the momentum shifted Trump's way, you could see his supporters getting more elated. And then suddenly, even when it hadn't been called yet, you knew Trump was going to win.

Olivia Nuzzi, political reporter, the Daily Beast: I'm 23, so I don't have anything really to compare it to. During the primary process, before it became evident that basically nobody knew anything any more about American politics, I was deferring to all of the so-called experts about what was likely to happen, and it became overwhelmingly clear midway through the primary that the experts had been rendered obsolete by Donald Trump. To realize that the inmates were completely running the asylum was sort of a jarring moment for me during the primary process.

Goldberg, the National Review: One of the reasons [the mainstream media is] in so much trouble right now when it comes to Trump is that they have a huge "cry wolf" problem. It was Daniel Schorr, in 1964, who said Barry Goldwater's trip to Europe after he had secured the nomination was really a clandestine trip to meet up with neo-Nazi elements. They have been doing this for a very long time. So when the press says that every Republican who's nominated, including Mitt Romney of all people, is a monster, and then the Republican party nominates a monster, you guys don't understand why half the country couldn't give a rat's a*s. That's on you guys to a considerable extent.

Repeat, Above journalists' quotes are originally from: (this article – *The Guardian's* **Accomplices or antagonists: how the media handled the Trump phenomenon** - source is taken from the Columbia Journalism Review reporting team **CJR's reporting team**: Shelley Hepworth, Vanessa Gezari, Kyle Pope, Carlett Spike, Cory Schouten, David Uberti and Pete Vernon
Source: https://www.theguardian.com/us-news/2016/nov/22/journalists-media-election-2016-donald-trump
CJR Oral History Source: http://www.cjr.org/special_report/trump_media_press_journalists.php

AUTHOR: Once again lets turn to the insightful post-Trump election words of a former Ad Executive now-turned *Hollywood Reporter* journalist who offers regular commentary to *USA Today,* the publication that called our 45th president of the United States a person "unfit for the Presidency."

Media has itself to blame for such an epic election fail, by Michael Wolff, *USA Today*, Money 7A, November 15, 2016

The extent of the media failure to anticipate or predict the election outcome, along with its concerted bet on a wholly different result, rather curiously resembles the banking industry's failure to anticipate the financial meltdown in 2007.

It's an institutional breakdown in the ability to do the basic job. Big banks should have hedged their bets against the subprime meltdown. Similarly, the media is supposed to keep enough of an open mind to the factors at hand to at least provide for the possibility of alternate outcomes.... This was not simple human error - 'Dewey Defeats Truman' – which might have been bad enough. For both the media and the financial industry, the failure to maintain objectivity came, in large part, from becoming uniquely vested in one outcome... The media ideologically aligned itself not just against Donald Trump but with the demographic groups that made up its audience. It found itself telling the stories its audience wanted to hear, a problem compounded by the fact that these were the stories the people in the media most wanted to hear.

Accomplices or antagonists: how the media handled the Trump phenomenon, by Ed Pilkington, *The Guardian,* November 22, 2016
Source: https://www.theguardian.com/us-news/2016/nov/22/journalists-media-election-2016-donald-trump

A third line of inquiry that is likely to run and run is whether the media, in its coastal bubble, failed to get to grips with the anger that was brewing right under its nose in the American heartlands. A flick of that argument was given in the missive sent by Arthur Sulzberger and Baquet, publisher and executive editor of the *New York Times*, to their readers soon after the election. "Did Donald Trump's sheer unconventionality lead us and other news outlets to underestimate his support among American voters?"

Answering his own question, Baquet told the *Guardian* US that the *Times* did in fact write extensively about anger in America in the run-up to the election, but adds that it's a good idea as an editor to be humble enough to ask oneself what questions should have been asked during the campaign.

Lies in guise of news, by Nicholas Kristof, *New York Times* International Edition, Opinion, November 14, 2016 page 16

"Rather, the problem with mainstream news sources is in part that we're out of touch with many of the ordinary voters whom we purport to care about."

Tommy Craggs, politics editor, Slate:
Source: https://www.theguardian.com/us-news/2016/nov/22/journalists-media-election-2016-donald-trump
I remember when [Trump] won the New York primary and essentially clinched the nomination. I said, "Watch, they're going to say – no matter what he does, no matter what he says – they're going to say he was more presidential." And that night, sure enough, *MSNBC, CNN,* they said Trump was more presidential, which just seems insane. He went up and didn't swallow his tie in front of everyone and as long as he didn't do that they were going to call him presidential. He could have gone up there and

danced the hoochie coochie and they would have said, "This is a welcome change in tone from Donald Trump."

AUTHOR: Here below in this excerpt from President Bill Clinton's 1995 State of the Union address, we see that his policies on immigration are a near carbon copy of the policies regarding illegal immigrants on which we heard President Trump campaign. And yet when Trump said these things he was branded as a racist. Is this a reflection of the major shift to the left in our country in the era spanning from 1995 to 2016?

Or is this simply a case where the sitting president can say one thing but the campaigning candidate dare not?

There's a third scenario: Because the Republican presidential candidate (now President) spoke out about immigration policy that flew in the face of the then incumbent Obama administration's, he was branded a racist. It's an easy trash-talk dismissal of an opposing viewpoint. Had Hillary Clinton echoed her husband's previous immigration policy stand during her campaign would she have been branded a racist by the liberal media? In 1995 her Democrat husband-president surely was not.

Here is an excerpt from Bill Clinton's 1995 State of the Union address: (C-Span)
VIDEO + transcripts https://www.c-span.org/video/?c4351026/clinton-1995-immigration-sotu

All Americans, not only in the States most heavily affected but in every place in this country, are rightly disturbed by the large numbers of illegal aliens entering our country. The jobs they hold might otherwise be held by citizens or legal immigrants. The public service they use impose burdens on our taxpayers. That's why our administration has moved aggressively to secure our borders more by hiring a record number of new border guards, by deporting twice as many criminal aliens as ever before, by cracking down on illegal hiring, by barring welfare benefits to illegal aliens. In the budget I will present to you, we will try to do more to speed the deportation of illegal aliens who are arrested for crimes, to better identify illegal aliens in the workplace as recommended by the commission headed by former Congresswoman Barbara Jordan. We are a nation of immigrants. But we are also a nation of laws. It is wrong and ultimately self-defeating for a nation of immigrants to permit the kind of abuse of our immigration laws we

have seen in recent years, and we must do
more to stop it.

Bill Clinton
The most important job
of our Government in
this new era is to
empower the American
people to succeed in the
global economy.
America has always
been a land of
opportunity, a land
where, if you work hard,
you can get ahead.
We've become a great
middle class country.
Middle class values
sustain us. We must
expand that middle
class and shrink the
under class, even as we
do everything we can to
support the millions of
Americans who are
already successful in the
new economy.

01:04:36

Media Malpractice? Media Bias and The 2016 Election, Written by Tom Westervelt and Raghavan
Mayur, *Investor's Business Daily*, Monday, 21 November 2016
http://www.tipponline.com/news/election-2016/792-media-malpractice-media-bias-and-the-2016-election

> **...After an election cycle that saw the news media so clearly bent on belittling
> and defeating a candidacy, media outlets must now conduct their own soul searching
> as they come to terms with an election result that caught them by surprise....**

"As Election Day demonstrated, the contentious 2016 presidential campaign witnessed a stunning
uprising of the people against the Washington establishment and political elite. This was not the only
revolt that transpired Nov. 8, however. Election Day also represented a victory of the American people
over the establishment news media, as they repudiated its liberal bias and attempt at influencing the
election.

Throughout the election cycle, Donald Trump and his supporters were derided for claiming that the mainstream media was "rigged" against the Republican candidate in favor of his opponent. But given the way Election Day unfolded, with Trump pulling off an upset victory despite being written off by much of the media, the allegations of media bias may not have been so far-fetched."

Evidence Of Media Bias
(same source: IBD - http://www.tipponline.com/news/election-2016/792-media-malpractice-media-bias-and-the-2016-election)

Even before Election Day, many asserted that Trump faced an unfair amount of negative press, as the media published story after story painting him as a racist, xenophobe and just about every other horrible name in the book. Case in point, throughout the campaign, the *Huffington Post* published the following editor's note at the end of stories about Mr. Trump:
(*Huffington Post - Editor's note*): *Donald Trump regularly incites political violence and is a serial liar, rampant xenophobe, racist, misogynist and birther who has repeatedly pledged to ban all Muslims — 1.6 billion members of an entire religion — from entering the U.S.*

AUTHOR: Then even *WaPo*, owned by Jeff Bezos eBay-billionaire-turned-newspaper-publisher, reported:

Source: IBD - http://www.tipponline.com/news/election-2016/792-media-malpractice-media-bias-and-the-2016-election

Further, following Hillary Clinton's health incident at a 9/11 commemoration ceremony, the venerable *Washington Post* published an article, entitled "The man who discovered CTE thinks Hillary Clinton may have been poisoned," which centered around a theory that Clinton may have been poisoned by Trump or Russian leader Vladimir Putin. The claim was made by Bennet Omalu, a forensic pathologist who had found that a number of NFL football players suffered from brain damage due to repeated blows to the head.

Instead of dismissing the poisoning claim as a conspiracy theory, the author appears to defend Omalu, as she wishes to remind readers that his "credentials and tenacity are well known." She also wants us to know that Putin was "implicated by a British inquiry" over the death of a former KGB operative, and that Trump "has expressed admiration for Putin."

Also, back in October, *Fox News* anchor Bill O'Reilly reported that at least three media organizations had "ordered their employees to destroy Donald Trump."

Source: IBD - http://www.tipponline.com/news/election-2016/792-media-malpractice-media-bias-and-the-2016-election
A majority of voters in the poll also felt that the news media tends to exert too much influence on U.S. elections. Overall, more than two-thirds of Americans (69%) believe that the news media wields too much of an influence on elections in the country. ...

It is not surprising, therefore, that most American voters lack confidence in the news media's ability to report accurately on the presidential candidates. According to an *Investor's Business Daily/*TIPP Poll conducted in September, more than two-thirds of registered voters (67%) reported that the media's reports on the candidates are often inaccurate, while only one-quarter trusted in the accuracy of its news stories.

The People's Repudiation Of Media Influence

Thus, despite the media's best efforts to defeat Trump through a barrage of negative news stories, most Americans appeared not to be swayed by media coverage.

Election Day provided the most definitive proof of both the media's bias against Trump and the people's repudiation of its attempts to influence the election narrative.

Heading into the day of the vote, most news outlets were confident that Clinton would become the 45th president of the United States, as they pointed to poll after poll showing the former secretary of state comfortably leading Trump. This coverage seemed to impact voters' sentiment regarding whom they expected to win the presidency. In the final installment of our daily IBD/TIPP Presidential Election Tracking Poll, released on the day of the election, nearly half of likely voters (46%) felt that Clinton would win the presidency, while only 24% reported that Trump would likely become president

Yet the media's negative coverage could not stifle Trump's supporters. As predicted in our final poll, which showed the Republican nominee with a 1.6-point lead over his rival, Trump stunned the media establishment and easily won the presidency.

New York Times' Soul Searching

...A question also needs to be asked regarding whether or not the Times would have delivered these "mea culpas" had Donald Trump lost the election...

In his recent article titled "*A 'Dewey Defeats Truman' Lesson for the Digital Age*," Times journalist Jim Rutenberg also admits that the media failed to "capture the boiling anger of a large portion of the American electorate that feels left behind by a selective recovery." He expresses his amazement at how frequently "the news media has missed the populist movements that have been rocking national politics since at least 2008."

Although Sulzberger and Rutenberg are admirable in their admission that the paper's election coverage got it wrong, they fail to acknowledge the fact that much of this coverage intentionally aimed to undermine Donald Trump's campaign by painting him as an unacceptable demagogue. Throughout the election cycle, even the hard news section of the *New York Times* went negative on candidate Trump.

(Read the Full Article: http://www.investors.com/politics/commentary/media-malpractice-media-bias-and-2016-election/)

Campaign 2016 Updates: Another newspaper that has long backed GOP candidates bucks Donald Trump, *LA Times*, Sept 29, 2016
Source: http://www.latimes.com/nation/politics/trailguide/la-na-live-updates-trailguide-don-t-vote-for-trump-says-usa-today-1475192834-htmlstory.html

Donald Trump campaigns Thursday in New Hampshire. Hillary Clinton swings into the battleground state of Iowa for an event in Des Moines.

- Employees at **Donald Trump's** California golf course say he wanted to fire women who weren't pretty enough.

- Trump leads Clinton in marriages, 3 to 1. That may not stop him from attacking hers

- Detroit News, another paper that has long backed GOP nominees, endorses **Gary Johnson**

- White supremacist **David Duke** on **Trump's** rise: "I'm winning."

- **Trump** has paid off the severance he owed to former campaign manager **Corey Lewandowski.**

Don't vote for Trump,' says *USA Today* in first presidential endorsement in its history, by Melanie Mason, *LA Times,* September 29, 2016

(AUTHOR: analyze that headline for a moment: ask yourself is this a presidential endorsement? Or is it an unequivocal presidential candidate rejection? Why is this headline using the word "endorsement?")

USA Today broke its 34-year tradition of not endorsing in a presidential race, publishing a scathing argument against voting for Donald Trump.

The editorial board unanimously found Trump "unfit for the presidency" and the editorial, published Thursday, goes on to list the reasons why, among them: his "erratic" behavior and his "checkered" business past.

The anti-Trump sentiment does not translate into an enthusiastic Clinton endorsement. The piece notes that although some editorial board members admire her record, others have "serious reservations about Clinton's sense of entitlement, her lack of candor and her extreme carelessness in handling classified information."

The editorial urges readers to follow their convictions, whether that means voting for Clinton, a third-party candidate, a write-in or by focusing on down-ticket races.

The piece ends on an unequivocal note.

"Whatever you do, however, resist the siren song of a dangerous demagogue. By all means vote, just not for Donald Trump."

Also on Thursday night, *USA Today* published an op-ed by Trump's vice-presidential pick, Indiana Gov. Mike Pence, who praises his running mate as leading a movement similar to the one catalyzed by Ronald Reagan.

The newspaper also published a companion piece to its editorial, explaining its reason for breaking precedent and weighing in on the presidential race this year.

Journalists need new rules after Trump, Marc Ambinder , *USA Today,* October 31, 2016
Source: http://www.usatoday.com/story/opinion/2016/10/31/journalists-truth-facts-trump-clinton-marc-ambinder/92847348/

How do you not take sides when one of those sides is so clearly wrong?

Many journalists dislike Donald Trump. They do. I can share this not-very-secret secret with you because I'm a few years removed from the practice, and I think this collective dislike can be channeled to help journalists do their jobs better in the future.

The level of animus cannot be explained by your average journalist's I-am-a-citizen-of-the-world disposition. Trump came from that world, even if he now tries to disavow it. It cannot be explained by media bias; liberal journalists have disliked and distrusted Hillary Clinton for decades. It cannot be explained, as Matt Lewis has suggested, by his free-wheeling, workaday speech patterns. They may be grating, but they aren't any different than the hundreds of non-writer humans that journalists deal with pleasantly every day.

Some of it, certainly, has to do with his character. Trump treats people badly and seems unbothered by it. But most of it, I think, has to do with the intense dissonance that he has created for journalists. Trump has made it much harder for them to cling to certain principles that form the spine (of, sic) the profession.

Here's a tried-and-true creed, straight from Journalism 101: Journalists should never take sides. But how do you not take sides when one of those sides is so clearly wrong?

Another: Journalists should not characterize political candidates as liars. But what happens when political candidates base their entire campaigns on very persuasive lies?

A third: Journalists should go to unfathomable lengths to avoid the appearance of bias, especially because their viewers, readers and listeners already mistrust their motives. But how do you avoid conveying the impression that you're rooting for one candidate (Clinton) when you try to cover the other candidate (Trump) in a way that reflects a shared, reality-based sensibility about the world?

Journalists are supposed to bend over backwards to treat unpopular points of view with respect. But at what point does that somersault confer legitimacy onto something that does not deserve it?

And since when did journalists become the designated signifiers of anything? Aren't they supposed to just observe and report?

AUTHOR: Journalist as observer. Journalist as stenographer. Journalist as unbiased reporter of events and facts. I would not readily use any of these definitions to describe the vast majority of our current mainstream media professionals.

Media has itself to blame for such an epic election fail, by Michael Wolff, *USA Today*, Money 7A, November 15, 2016

"Jill Abramson, the former editor of the *NY Times* and now a freelance advocate for good journalism, took to Twitter to excuse her former employer: 'Great institution falsely blamed for getting it wrong. Job of @nytimes is to inform and hold power accountable. Did both magnificently.'

In fact, while those might be nice results, the actual job is to be accurate. Getting it wrong ought to be as dismal a result as when a bank loses money, with someone called on the carpet. When structural flaws in method and in intelligence make it increasingly difficult (if not impossible) to get it right, that's an institutional crisis – a kind of bankruptcy."

Trump vs. the media: did his tactics mortally wound the fourth estate? by Ed Pilkington, *The Guardian*, November 22, 2016
Source: https://www.theguardian.com/media/2016/nov/22/election-2016-donald-trump-media-coverage

Jorge Ramos, the lead news anchor at Univision, predicted on election day that Trump would lose because he had turned his back on the Spanish-language media. Didn't happen – almost one in three Hispanics backed him, to Ramos's bafflement …

Jay Rosen, who teaches journalism at New York University and whose blog PressThink.org has been a widely cited resource on the fraught relationship between Trump and the press in 2016, sees the DC hotel debacle as a seminal moment. "That's when people in the campaign press corp got disgusted not just with Trump's mendacity and manipulation but at themselves for playing along with it. That turned the worm."

Media has itself to blame for such an epic election fail, by Michael Wolff, *USA Today* International Edition, Money 7A, November 15, 2016

The New York Times, the *Washington Post*, the *Huffington Post, CNN*, even *Buzzfeed* are perhaps too big to fail – at least in a journalistic, if not financial, sense. No one is going to hold them accountable for painting a picture of reality that was not real, indeed for trying to use their influence to bend reality.

No one need take responsibility. Leaders at the the *Times* and *CNN*, in fact, issued rousing encomiums to the greatness of their election coverage and the accomplishments of their staffs. Bad calls, even gross misunderstandings of the fundamental currents of the time, being merely yesterday's news and hence easily forgotten. In a time of deep media unpopularity, it would surely have been wiser and more honorable for these leaders to have fallen on their swords. ....

But the media, like the banks, will not so easily recover from what everybody knows: Aligning lock-step behind a political and cultural outlook, it produced for almost 18 months, with hardly a deviation anywhere in its ranks, a narrative which was off about 180 degrees from what was actually occurring and from the story that would ultimately unfold.

AUTHOR: There is an old wives' tale that recalls the arrival of Captain Cook's ship, Endeavor, to Australian shores. It was popularized in the movie, *What The Bleep Do We Know?* (though its veracity has since been challenged). In this tale it says that the Australian aborigines could not see the ship though it was passing just offshore. Were they blind? No. They had perfect vision. They just could not see the ship. Why? It is explained by psychologists (some would claim, pseudo-science) that we cannot see, are blind to, in fact, that which is outside our habitual framework of reality. Whether this tale is true or not, it offers some sort of salve/explanation as to why the liberal mainstream media ignored half the population of America during and leading up to our 2016 presidential election.

Have we been pulled into a cocoon by social media? By Jenna Wortham, *NY Times* International Edition, page 8 (printed originally in the *NY Times Magazine*)

What happens when we would rather look inward? I have found something of an answer in a short story called, 'The Great Silence,' by Ted Chiang, about humankind's search for signs of alien life. The story is narrated by a parrot in Arecibo, Puetro Rico, home to one of the largest radio telescopes in the world.

'Their desire to make a connection is so strong that they've created an ear capable of hearing across the universe,' the creature begins. 'But I and my fellow parrots are right here. Why aren't they listening to our voices?'

The paradox is not to be missed: We are more interested in locating alien species than understanding the humanity among the species we already live with. The story ends on a somber note:

'Human activity has brought my kind to the brink of extinction,' the narrator explains. 'They didn't do it maliciously. They just weren't paying attention.'

Chapter 7

The Rise In Popularity of Fake News

I disapprove of what you say, but I will defend to the death your right to say it.

- Evelyn Beatrice Hall, Ch. 7:Helvétius: The Contradictio n(1906), p. 199. Often misattributed to Voltaire.

AUTHOR: Sponsored Content and Native Ads – just another name for Fake News.

Let's be real, there's nothing new about fake news. As a child in the 70's I recall standing in line at the grocery store with my mother and reading the tabloid press, ones like *The National Enquirer* and so forth, announcing which celebrity the just-landed extra-terrestrial little green men debarking from the UFO had mated with that week. And other such outlandish reports. People did not pay much attention to these stories then, outside of their momentary entertainment quotient, and people, I would argue, do not pay much attention to these kinds of stories now.

So, this sudden public and establishment media outcry about fake news having overtaken social media during the 2016 presidential election cycle feels a bit orchestrated. I would also charge that it is being used as something of a smokescreen to deflect any culpability from the mainstream corporate media in regards to their wholehearted adoption in recent years of Native Ads and Sponsored Content. Those two terms, Native Ads and Sponsored Content, are just media-generated jargon that refer to paid advertisements that are made to look like, and presented as, unbiased editorial content. The *NYT* went so far as to create its own stand-alone agency within their company that generates this sponsored content rather than outsourcing it any longer to ad agencies. That in-house "ad agency" is called T Brand Studio and it's been generating gobs of native ads for years now.

My conclusion then, so far, about this post-election fake news issue is that it is being blown up into a significant national issue only now because it is expedient for the losing Democratic party and their candidate to do so – now. Whereas the reality is that there is absolutely nothing new about fake news and neither is it the proprietary domain of the left nor the right.

How Sponsored Content Is Becoming King in a Facebook World, by John Herrman, *New York Times*, July 24, 2016
Source: http://www.nytimes.com/2016/07/25/business/sponsored-content-takes-larger-role-in-media-companies.html?_r=0

In recent years, publications large and small have invested in teams to make sponsored content — written stories, videos or podcasts that look and feel like journalistic content — hoping to make up for declines in conventional advertising. To varying degrees, they have succeeded.

Younger companies like *Vice* and *BuzzFeed* have built whole businesses around the concept. *The Atlantic* expects three-quarters of its digital ad revenue to come from sponsored content this year. *Slate*, the web publisher, says that about half of its ad revenue comes from native ads, as sponsored content is also called, and the other half from traditional banner or display ads. Many major newspapers, including *The New York Times*, have declared sponsored content to be an important part of their strategies.

But as the relationship between publishers and social platforms like <u>Facebook</u> grows closer — and as more straightforward forms of advertising are devalued by ad-blocking and industry automation, the role, and definition, of sponsored content has shifted. Now, publishers, social media companies and advertisers are negotiating new relationships. Audiences have migrated away from news websites and toward Facebook and other social media destinations, ...

Donald Trump Clung to Birther Lie for Years and Still Isn't Apologetic, by Michael Barbaro, *New York Times*, Sept. 16, 2016
Source: <u>http://www.nytimes.com/2016/09/17/us/politics/donald-trump-obama-birther.html?_r=1</u>

What he could do — and what he did do — was talk about it, uninhibitedly, on social media, where dark rumors flourish in 140-character bursts and, inevitably, find a home with those who have no need for facts and whose suspicions can never be allayed.

AUTHOR: What exactly is the U.S.'s legal position on freedom of speech and expression? During the election campaign we often heard accusations by one candidate (Hillary) of the other (Trump) that his words were "inciting racism, hatred and violence." That phrase is significant because it is the one tactic you can try to use to suppress the words of an opponent or an accuser in our country. BUT, in order to have legal recourse, you must prove it – not just the inciting to violence but more specifically the intention to produce "imminent lawless action." And this couldn't be done during the campaign, hence speech flowed freely and much of it unfiltered, thanks to adept use of social media platforms.

To get a clear picture of the law and where it stands in regards to freedom of speech and 1st Amendment rights in the U.S., let's take a look first this ACLU position paper, excerpts of which are printed below.

ACLU - position paper on Freedom of Speech
Source: https://www.aclu.org/other/freedom-expression-aclu-position-paper

Finally, in 1969, in Brandenberg v. Ohio, the Supreme Court struck down the conviction of a Ku Klux Klan member, and established a new standard: Speech can be suppressed only if it is intended, and likely to produce, "imminent lawless action." Otherwise, even speech that advocates violence is protected. The Brandenberg standard prevails today. ...

...Government can limit some protected speech by imposing "time, place and manner" restrictions. This is most commonly done by requiring permits for meetings, rallies and demonstrations. But a permit cannot be unreasonably withheld, nor can it be denied based on content of the speech. That would be what is called viewpoint discrimination – and *that is unconstitutional.*

Twitter suspends major alt-right accounts, by Amar Toor, *The Verge*, November 16 2016)
Source: http://www.theverge.com/2016/11/16/13648922/twitter-suspends-alt-right-accounts-richard-spencer-trump-

Among the users suspended this week is Richard Spencer, head of the National Policy Institute, a white nationalist think tank that, according to its website, is "dedicated to the heritage, identity, and future of people of European descent in the United States." Spencer's personal verified account was suspended, as were those of the National Policy Institute and his magazine, *Radix Journal*. Other suspended alt-right Twitter users include Paul Town, Pax Dickinson, Ricky Vaughn and John Rivers.

In an interview with *The Daily Caller*, Spencer   *"CORPORATE STALINISM"*
described Twitter's move as "corporate Stalinism."
"Twitter is trying to airbrush the alt-right out of existence," he told the website. "They're clearly afraid. They will fail!" In a YouTube video posted online Tuesday, he said that online "execution squads" were targeting the alt-right,....

In July, Twitter banned notorious troll Milo Yiannopoulos after he encouraged his followers to tweet racist messages to *Ghostbusters* actress Leslie Jones, though before Tuesday, the site had never suspended alt-right accounts en masse. The suspensions also come after Trump's controversial decision to appoint Steve Bannon as chief strategist in his administration. Bannon, the executive chairman of the right-wing site *Breitbart News*, served as Trump's campaign CEO.

Facebook, In Cross-hairs After Election, Is Said to Question Its Influence, by Mike Isaac, *New York Times* International Edition, November 12 2016

"Of all the content on Facebook, more than 99% of what people see is authentic. Only a very small amount is fake news and hoaxes," Mr. Zuckerberg wrote. "Overall, this makes it extremely unlikely hoaxes changed the outcome of this election in one direction or the other."
He added - "I am confident we can find ways for our community to tell us what content is most meaningful, but I believe we must be extremely cautious about becoming arbiters of truth ourselves."

(Facebook has 1.8 billion users)
"Facebook has been in the eye of the post election storm for the past few days, embroiled in accusations that it helped spread misinformation and fake news stories that influenced the way the American electorate voted. ... Even as Facebook has outwardly defended itself as a nonpartisan information source – Mark Zuckerberg, Facebook's chief executive, said at a news conference on Thursday that Facebook's affecting the election was a 'pretty crazy idea' – many company executives and employees have been asking one another if, or how, they shaped the minds, opinions and votes of Americans.

AUTHOR: Of course a business in America has the discretion to allow onto its platform or into its doors whomever it chooses. But Twitter, by deleting alt-right accounts based solely on their expressed viewpoints, has now moved itself squarely into the camp of propagandists. For a social sharing medium that once prided itself on being the self-described "free speech platform of the free speech party," its recent actions run counter to that. The negative reaction to this kind of censorship by its community of users mounted over several years and ended up sparking the creation of a new, similar micro-blog social sharing site called Gab. Gab.ai, created in August 2016 is a new Twitter-style freedom of speech-focused social media network.

Twitter suspends several accounts in alt-right purge, by James Rogers, *Fox News*, November 17, 2016
Source: Fox News http://www.foxnews.com/tech/2016/11/17/twitter-suspends-several-accounts-in-alt-right-purge.html
Twitter has suspended a number of prominent accounts associated with the so-called "alt-right" movement, in an apparent purge...
The alt-right, short for "alternative right," is a term applied to a mostly unaffiliated group of individuals and organizations who reject mainstream conservatism.

Twitter Holocaust, SPLC Has Dozens of Alt-Right Accounts Deleted, Then Brags About It, by Ethan Ralph, *The Ralph Retort*, November 16, 2016
Source: http://theralphretort.com/twitter-holocaust-splc-dozens-alt-right-accounts-deleted-brags-11016016/

Twitter has entered a new phase in their war against free expression. The same place that once claimed to represent the "free speech wing of the free speech party" has now decided to wipe out numerous alt-right accounts at the behest of the Southern Poverty Law Center, a group which claims expertise when it comes to so-called hate speech (when in reality they're just a far-left advocacy group). I've long loved Twitter, and somehow I've escaped the death squads so far, but things don't look very good for the future.

Ethan Ralph

@TheRalphRetort

Twitter intended to purge alt-right accounts as part of a Hillary victory celebration. Now, it's revenge. 12:59 am 16 November 2016

I don't understand how they think this is going to help the service. Instead of finding ways to keep new users involved with Twitter, or teaching them how it works, they've decided to cull power users at the behest of the SPLC. It would be different if they decided to crack down on the left as well, although I would still be against it.

Twitter suspends alt-right accounts, *by Jessica Guynn, USA Today,* November 16, 2016
Source: http://www.usatoday.com/story/tech/news/2016/11/15/twitter-suspends-alt-right-accounts/93943194/

> Twitter suspended high-profile accounts associated with the alt-right movement, the same day the social media service said it would crack down on hate speech.

> Among those suspended was Richard Spencer

Twitter on Tuesday removed Spencer's verified account, @RichardBSpencer, that of his think tank, the NatioFanal Policy Institute @npiamerica, and his online magazine @radixjournal.

"I am alive physically but digitally speaking there has been execution squads across the alt right," he said. "There is a great purge going on and they are purging people based on their views." - Spencer

In a statement, Twitter said: "The Twitter Rules prohibit targeted abuse and harassment, and we will suspend accounts that violate this policy."

It declined to comment specifically on the suspensions, which included the accounts of Paul Town, Pax Dickinson, Ricky Vaughn and John Rivers. Twitter was the platform of choice for the campaign of President-elect Donald Trump and the alt-right political movement that embraced him... For years, Twitter billed itself as "the free speech wing of the free speech party."

Would Facebook or Twitter Ever Ban President Trump? By Will Oremus, *Slate*, Nov 28, 2016
http://www.slate.com/articles/technology/technology/2016/11/would_facebook_or_twitter_ban_preside
nt_trump.html

Could the president of the United States ever get suspended or banned from a major social network? The answer: It depends on the network. Facebook has indicated that it will not apply its normal community standards to posts from President-elect Trump, given their newsworthiness and the widespread popular support for his views. But Twitter told *Slate* that no one is exempt from its rules—not even the president. ...

CEO Mark Zuckerberg. "When we review reports of content that may violate our policies, we take context into consideration," a Facebook spokesperson said via email. "That context can include the value of political discourse." The spokesperson noted that this approach is not Trump-specific.

Still, the *Wall Street Journal* reported in October that some Facebook employees had pressed for Trump's Facebook page to be suspended for posts that they believed violated the company's community standards on hate speech, including posts that called for a ban on Muslims entering the United States. But Zuckerberg decided in December that it would be inappropriate to interfere with a major-party candidate's political posts, the *Wall Street Journal* reported.

Zuckerberg himself clarified his stand in an onstage interview with David Kirkpatrick at the Techonomy conference on Nov. 10. Asked about his decision not to take action against Trump's page, Zuckerberg said:

> Our real goal is to reflect what our community wants. That kind of content, we would have thought previously that would make a lot of people feel uncomfortable, and people wouldn't want that. But at the point where the person who's elected president of the United States is expressing that opinion and has 60 million people who are followers, then the question is. OK, I think that that is mainstream political discourse that I think we need to be pretty careful about saying that that's not a reasonable [inaudible].

AUTHOR: The alternative GAB.ai launched in the late summer of 2016 was profiled in several media outlets, including on Breitbart.com. GAB bills itself as being a Twitter-like social media platform dedicated to free speech.

Meet The CEO of GAB, The Free Speech Alternative to Twitter, by Charlie Nash, *Breitbart.com*,
August 23, 2016
Source: http://www.breitbart.com/tech/2016/08/23/meet-the-ceo-of-gab-the-free-speech-alternative-to-twitter/
Charlie Nash: Censorship has been rampant on social networks such as Facebook and Twitter for quite some time now. What was the final straw that pushed you into developing Gab.ai?
Andrew Torba: If I had to pick a single event that pushed me over the edge to take action, I would have to say it was the suppression of conservative sources and stories by the incredibly biased Facebook Trending Topics team.
Many of us don't realize just how much power and influence the News Feed and Trending Topics products have on our psychological understanding of the world around us. There are hundreds of

millions of people who get their main source of news and information from a handful of companies in one of the most progressively liberal cities in the world, it's time for a change.

AUTHOR: Below are a random selection of quotes and thoughts on freedom of speech as historically documented prior to the formation of and throughout our country's history. Most of them have been culled quite simply from Wikipedia, illustrating that these are thoughts, building blocks of our modern society, that are still easily found on the internet and in libraries. Let's all pray, as well as take action, so that this continues to be the case in our great nation for generations to come.

Freedom of Speech : Quotes   https://en.wikiquote.org/wiki/Freedom_of_speech

Without Freedom of Thought, there can be no such Thing as Wisdom; and no such Thing as publick Liberty, without Freedom of Speech; which is the Right of every Man, as far as by it, he does not hurt or control the Right of another. And this is the only Check it ought to suffer, and the only bounds it ought to know. This sacred Privilege is to essential to free Governments, that the Security of Property, and the Freedom of Speech always go together; and in those wretched Countries where a Man cannot call his Tongue his own, he can scarce call any Thing else his own. Whoever would overthrow the Liberty of a Nation, must begin by subduing the Fteeness [sic!] of Speech; a *Thing* terrible to Publick Traytors. Cato's Letters, <u>John Trenchard</u> and <u>Thomas Gordon</u> (Letter Number 15, *Freedom of Speech, That the Same is inseparable from Publick Liberty*, February 4, 1720).

Give me the liberty to know, to utter, and to argue freely according to conscience, above all liberties. John Milton, <u>Areopagitica: A Speech for the Liberty of Unlicens'd Printing, to the Parliament of England</u> (published November 23, 1644).

Freedom of speech is the great bulwark of liberty; they prosper and die together: And it is the terror of traitors and oppressors, and a barrier against them. It produces excellent writers, and encourages men of fine genius. Cato's Letters, <u>John Trenchard</u> and <u>Thomas Gordon</u> (Letter Number 15, *Of Freedom of Speech, That the Same is inseparable from Publick Liberty*, February 4, 1720).

Without Freedom of Thought, there can be no such Thing as Wisdom; and no such Thing as publick Liberty, without Freedom of Speech. Benjamin Franklin, letter from "Silence Dogood," no. 8, printed in *The New-England Courant, Boston, Massachusetts (July 9, 1722). Franklin, writing under the pseudonym Silence Dogood, was quoting the London Journal, no. 80, February 4, 1720/1;*

For if Men are to be precluded from offering their Sentiments on a matter, which may involve the most serious and alarming consequences, that can invite the consideration of Mankind, reason is of no use to us; the freedom of Speech may be taken away, and, dumb and silent we may be led, like sheep, to the Slaughter. George Washington, address to the officers of the army, Newburgh, New York (March 15, 1783); reported in John C. Fitzpatrick, ed, *The Writings of George Washington* (1938), vol. 26, p. 225.

The free communication of thoughts and of opinions is one of the most precious rights of man: any citizen thus may speak, write, print freely, except to respond to the abuse of this liberty, in the cases determined by the law. - Declaration of the Rights of Man and of the Citizen (1789), Article XI

I would rather be exposed to the inconveniences attending too much liberty, than those attending too small a degree of it. Thomas Jefferson to Archibald Stuart, Philadelphia, December 23, 1791

A popular Government without popular information, or the means of acquiring it, is but a Prologue to a Farce or a Tragedy, or perhaps both. Knowledge will forever govern ignorance: And a people who mean to be their own Governors, must arm themselves with the power which knowledge gives. James Madison, Letter to W.T. Barry (1822-08-04)

And I honor the man who is willing to sink
Half his present repute for the freedom to think,
And, when he has thought, be his cause strong or weak,
Will risk t'other half for the freedom to speak.
•James Russell Lowell, *A Fable for Critics* (1848), Pt. V - *Cooper*, st. 3.

•No law shall be passed restraining the free expression of opinion, or restricting the right to speak, write or print freely on any subject whatever.
•*Oregon Constitution*, (1857), Article I, Section 8.

If any opinion is compelled to silence, that opinion may, for aught we can certainly know, be true. To deny this is to assume our own infallibility. ... Though the silenced opinion be an error, it may. and very commonly does, contain a portion of truth; and since the general or prevailing opinion on any subject is rarely or never the whole truth, it is only by the collision of adverse opinions that the remainder of the truth has any chance of being supplied ... Even if the received opinion be not only true, but the whole truth; unless it is suffered to be, and actually is, vigorously and earnestly contested, it will, by most of those who receive it, be held in the manner of a prejudice, with little comprehension [of] or feeling [for] its rational grounds.
•John Stuart Mill, *On Liberty*, (1859).

I would not wish to live in a world where I could not express my honest opinions. Men who deny to others the right of speech are not fit to live with honest men.
I deny the right of any man, of any number of men, of any church, of any State, to put a padlock on the lips — to make the tongue a convict. I passionately deny the right of the Herod of authority to kill the children of the brain. Robert G. Ingersoll, in an appeal to the jury in the trial of C.B. Reynolds for blasphemy (May 1887).

I would defend the freedom of speech. And why? Because no attack can be answered by force, no argument can be refuted by a blow, or by imprisonment, or by fine. You may imprison the man, but the argument is free; you may fell the man to the earth, but the statement stands.
•Robert G. Ingersoll, in an appeal to the jury in the trial of C.B. Reynolds for blasphemy (May 1887).

•Without free speech no search for Truth is possible; without free speech no discovery of Truth is useful; without free speech progress is checked, and the nations no longer march forward towards the nobler life which the future holds for man. Better a thousandfold abuse of free speech than denial of free speech. The abuse dies in a day; the denial slays the life of the people and entombs the hope of the race.

•Charles Bradlaugh, Speech at Hall of Science *c.*1880 quoted in <u>An Autobiography</u> of Annie Besant; reported in *Edmund Fuller, Thesaurus of Quotations*(1941), p. 398; reported as unverified in *Respectfully Quoted: A Dictionary of Quotations* (1989).

I disapprove of what you say, but I will defend to the death your right to say it. - Evelyn Beatrice Hall, Ch. 7: *Helvetius: The Contradiction*(1906), p. 199. Often misattributed to Voltaire.

•Though these words are regularly attributed to Voltaire, they were first used by Evelyn Beatrice Hall, writing under the pseudonym of Stephen G Tallentyre in *The Friends of Voltaire* (1906), as a summation of Voltaire's beliefs on freedom of thought and expression.[13]
•Another possible source for the quote was proposed by Norbert Guterman, editor of "A Book of French Quotations," who noted a letter to M. le Riche (6 February 1770) in which Voltaire is quoted as saying: "Monsieur l'abbé, I detest what you write, but I would give my life to make it possible for you to continue to write" (*"Monsieur l'abbé, je déteste ce que vous écrivez, mais je donnerai ma vie pour que vous puissiez continuer à écrire"*). This remark, however, does not appear in the letter.

We must not confuse dissent with disloyalty. We must remember always that accusation is not proof and that conviction depends upon evidence and due process of law. We will not walk in fear, one of another. We will not be driven by fear into an age of unreason, if we dig deep in our history and our doctrine, and remember that we are not descended from fearful men – not from men who feared to write, to speak, to associate, and to defend causes that were, for the moment, unpopular.
– Edward R. Murrow Source: https://www.goodreads.com/author/quotes/178884.Edward_R_Murrow

AUTHOR: It's always useful to put into historical context current events. In the below cited ACLU position paper, it is made clear that this challenge to our freedom of speech and First Amendment rights that our country is currently experiencing has historical precedent. Thus far, historically speaking, we have successfully been able to overcome these challenges in the United States. It is up to us to remain ever vigilant, and never more so than today.

The ACLU's Position Paper
Source: https://www.aclu.org/other/freedom-expression-aclu-position-paper

THE FIRST AMENDMENT IGNORED

Early Americans enjoyed great freedom compared to citizens of other nations. Nevertheless, once in power, even the Constitution's framers were guilty of overstepping the First Amendment they had so recently adopted. In 1798, during the French-Indian War, Congress passed the Alien and Sedition Act, which made it a crime for anyone to publish "any false, scandalous and malicious writing" against the government. It was used by the then-dominant Federalist Party to prosecute prominent Republican newspaper editors during the late 18th century.

Throughout the 19th century, sedition, criminal anarchy and criminal conspiracy laws were used to suppress the speech of abolitionists, religious minorities, suffragists, labor organizers, and pacifists. In Virginia prior to the Civil War, for example, anyone who "by speaking or writing maintains that owners have no right of property in slaves" was subject to a one-year prison sentence.

The early 20th century was not much better. In 1912, feminist Margaret Sanger was arrested for giving a lecture on birth control. Trade union meetings were banned and courts routinely granted injunctions prohibiting strikes and other labor protests. Violators were sentenced to prison. Peaceful protesters opposing U. S. entry into World War I were jailed for expressing their opinions. In the early 1920s, many states outlawed the display of red or black flags, symbols of communism and anarchism. In 1923, author Upton Sinclair was arrested for trying to read the text of the First Amendment at a union rally. Many people were arrested merely for membership in groups regarded as "radical" by the government. It was in response to the excesses of this period that the ACLU was founded in 1920.

Also from the ACLU's position paper on Freedom of Speech:
Source: https://www.aclu.org/other/freedom-expression-aclu-position-paper

Freedom of speech, of the press, of association, of assembly and petition -- this set of guarantees, protected by the First Amendment, comprises what we refer to as freedom of expression. The Supreme Court has written that this freedom is "the matrix, the indispensable condition of nearly every other form of freedom." Without it, other fundamental rights, like the right to vote, would wither and die.

But in spite of its "preferred position" in our constitutional hierarchy, the nation's commitment to freedom of expression has been tested over and over again. Especially during times of national stress, like war abroad or social upheaval at home, people exercising their First Amendment rights have been censored, fined, even jailed. Those with unpopular political ideas have always borne the brunt of government repression. It was during WWI -- hardly ancient history -- that a person could be jailed just for giving out anti-war leaflets. Out of those early cases, modern First Amendment law evolved. Many struggles and many cases later, ours is the most speech-protective country in the world.

The path to freedom was long and arduous. It took nearly 200 years to establish firm constitutional limits on the government's power to punish "seditious" and "subversive" speech. Many people suffered along the way, such as labor leader Eugene V. Debs, who was sentenced to 10 years in prison under the Espionage Act just for telling a rally of peaceful workers to realize they were "fit for something better than slavery and cannon fodder."

Cont'd From The ACLU – Position Paper on Freedom of Expression

WHAT DOES "PROTECTED SPEECH" INCLUDE?

First Amendment protection is not limited to "pure speech" -- books, newspapers, leaflets, and rallies. It also protects "symbolic speech" -- nonverbal expression whose purpose is to communicate ideas. In its 1969 decision in Tinker v. Des Moines, the Court recognized the right of public school students to wear black armbands in protest of the Vietnam War. In 1989 (Texas v. Johnson) and again in 1990 (U.S. v. Eichman), the Court struck down government bans on "flag desecration." Other examples of protected symbolic speech include works of art, T-shirt slogans, political buttons, music lyrics and theatrical performances.

Government can limit some protected speech by imposing "time, place and manner" restrictions. This is most commonly done by requiring permits for meetings, rallies and demonstrations. But a permit cannot be unreasonably withheld, nor can it be denied based on content of the speech. That would be what is called viewpoint discrimination – and that is unconstitutional.

When a protest crosses the line from speech to action, the government can intervene more aggressively. Political protesters have the right to picket, to distribute literature, to chant and to engage passersby in debate. But they do not have the right to block building entrances or to physically harass people.

FREE SPEECH FOR HATEMONGERS?

The ACLU has often been at the center of controversy for defending the free speech rights of groups that spew hate, such as the Ku Klux Klan and the Nazis. But if only popular ideas were protected, we wouldn't need a First Amendment. History teaches that the first target of government repression is never the last. If we do not come to the defense of the free speech rights of the most unpopular among us, even if their views are antithetical to the very freedom the First Amendment stands for, then no one's liberty will be secure. In that sense, all First Amendment rights are "indivisible."

Censoring so-called hate speech also runs counter to the long-term interests of the most frequent victims of hate: racial, ethnic, religious and sexual minorities. We should not give the government the power to decide which opinions are hateful, for history has taught us that government is more apt to use this power to prosecute minorities than to protect them. As one federal judge has put it, tolerating hateful speech is "the best protection we have against any Nazi-type regime in this country."

At the same time, freedom of speech does not prevent punishing conduct that intimidates, harasses, or threatens another person, even if words are used. Threatening phone calls, for example, are not constitutionally protected.

SPEECH & NATIONAL SECURITY

The Supreme Court has recognized the government's interest in keeping some information secret, such as wartime troop deployments. But the Court has never actually upheld an injunction against speech on national security grounds. Two lessons can be learned from this historical fact. First, the amount of speech that can be curtailed in the interest of national security is very limited. And second, the government has historically overused the concept of "national security" to shield itself from criticism, and to discourage public discussion of controversial policies or decisions.

In 1971, the publication of the "Pentagon Papers" by the *New York Times* brought the conflicting claims of free speech and national security to a head. The Pentagon Papers, a voluminous secret history and analysis of the country's involvement in Vietnam, was leaked to the press. When the *Times* ignored the government's demand that it cease publication, the stage was set for a Supreme Court decision. In the landmark *U.S. v. New York Times* case, the Court ruled that the government could not, through "prior restraint," block publication of any material unless it could prove that it would "surely" result in "direct, immediate, and irreparable" harm to the nation. This the government failed to prove, and the public was given access to vital information about an issue of enormous importance.

The public's First Amendment "right to know" is essential to its ability to fully participate in democratic decision-making. As the Pentagon Papers case demonstrates, the government's claims of "national security" must always be closely scrutinized to make sure they are valid.

Committee to Protect Journalists: President Trump would be threat to press freedom (*USA Today*, October 13, 2016)
Source: http://www.usatoday.com/story/news/politics/onpolitics/2016/10/13/committee-protect-journalists-president-trump-would-threaten-press-freedom/92002796/

As Donald Trump gave one of his strongest condemnations of the press during the election cycle, the Committee to Protect Journalists issued a public warning Thursday that a Trump win "would represent a threat to press freedom."

> 'Donald Trump, through his words and actions as a candidate for president of the United States, has consistently betrayed First Amendment values. On October 6, CPJ's board of directors passed a resolution declaring Trump an unprecedented threat to the rights of journalists and to CPJ's ability to advocate for press freedom around the world.
> 'Since the beginning of his candidacy, Trump has insulted and vilified the press and has made his opposition to the media a centerpiece of his campaign. Trump has routinely labeled the press as 'dishonest' and 'scum' and singled out individual news organizations and journalists.

CPJ is a nonprofit organization that reports on press freedoms around the world.

"This is not about picking sides in an election. This is recognizing that a Trump presidency represents a threat to press freedom unknown in modern history," CPJ wrote.

AUTHOR: As a journalist I have had several discussions with the CPJ over the years, especially during the Obama Administration. I have found them to be a politicized group who cherry-pick their battles in defending journalists and from which countries. It is often easier to keep the world's focus on the heinous abuses and jailings of journalists abroad in countries like Egypt, Iran, Turkey and China than to acknowledge anything askance or egregious happening within our own borders.

I also must add that if Trump and his supporters are such a threat to freedom of speech in the United States than why is it only the right-leaning journalists' and bloggers' Twitter accounts that are getting deleted? Why was there a discussion about only Trump's facebook page getting deleted and not Hillary's? Which of the two candidates, after all, was under FBI investigation for possible illegal conduct for much of the presidential campaign cycle? (Hint: It wasn't Trump).

Facebook shouldn't check facts, *New York Times*, International Edition, November 29th, 2016, pg. 16
Op-Ed by Jessica Lessin, founder and Chief Executive of *The Information*

"We finally got a grudging mea culpa from Mark Zuckerberg: an admission that fake news is a significant problem that his social network must help solve.

But as a journalist who has been covering the inner workings of the technology industry for more than a decade, I find the calls for Facebook to accept broad responsibility for fact-checking the news, including by hiring editors and reporters, deeply unsettling.... hiring editors to enforce accuracy – or even promising to enforce accuracy by partnering with third parties – would create the perception that Facebook is policing the 'truth,' and that is worrisome.

...One thing is clear to anyone who has worked in a newsroom: not all fact checking decisions are black and white. Did the pope endorse Mr. Trump? He did not. But did the F.B.I. reopen the Hillary Clinton email investigation? Well, that's a little tougher. Although major news outlets like *CNN* said that it had, the agency didn't reopen the inquiry, which would have been a far more significant move than what it did do (which was to take a look at newly discovered emails to see if it should reconsider its decision to close the case).

Erroneous reporting by established organizations is a bigger threat than fabricated stories, and far more rampant.

...I'm not comfortable trusting the truth to one gatekeeper that has a mission and a fiduciary duty to increase advertising revenue, especially when revenue is tied more to engagement than information....

The second reason I am fearful of Facebook as fact checker is what it will do to journalism. If you don't believe that Facebook's policies could sway the news industry, you haven't been paying attention over the past five years. Publications have been suckered into tweaking their content and their business models to try to live off the traffic Facebook sends them. They've favored Facebook clicks over their core readers, and are no closer to addressing plummeting print revenues.

What would happen if the distribution of their articles on Facebook was tied to submitting data about their sources or conforming to some site-endorsed standards about what constitutes a trustworthy news source?

...I simply don't trust Facebook, or any one company, with the responsibility for determining what is true."

Liberal definition of Freedom of Speech
"Liberals Love Free Speech: So Long As You Agree With Them." – anonymous

"The heretics of today are the heros of tomorrow. " - E. Y. Harburg, the lyricist of *Somewhere Over The Rainbow*, song from *The Wizard of Oz*

AUTHOR:
When mainstream media is misreporting facts and miscalculating outcomes to presage their wished-for results, what distinguishes it from "fake" news?

US Media to Get Even After Clinton's Loss Amid Crackdown on 'Fake News' Sites, *Sputnik News,* published November 23, 2016
Source: https://sputniknews.com/world/201611231047736563-us-corporate-media-fake-news/

The IT billionaires in Silicon Valley and elsewhere and the corporate mainstream media are reacting to Hillary Clinton's defeat in the US election by seeking to shut down genuine free speech, Wall Street analyst and Trends Research Institute head Gerald Celente told Sputnik.

WASHINGTON (Sputnik) — According to Celente, media are "taking cheap shots at getting even by claiming it was fake news and not that people were disgusted with the Clintons."
Merrimack College Assistant Professor Melissa Zimdars, a self-proclaimed feminist activist, recently created a list of the allegedly fake news sites. The corporate media extensively covered the list, which reportedly serves as the starting point in creting (sic) a nerative (sic) suitable to censor alternative and independent media in the United States, including the *Daily Wire, Zero Hedge, Breitbart, WND. Red State* and *Infowars*.

Celente recalled that Google had already been accused of repeatedly manipulating search results to favor Hillary Clinton earlier this year. Now Mark Zuckerberg and other Silicon Valley IT billionaires who had enthusiastically backed Clinton are refusing to accept that they had lost fair and square in the established US political process.

"The Zuckerbergs, and the rest of the Silicon Valley billionaires— they lost and payback is tough to take," Celente stated. In their accusations that the independent and alternative media were peddling fake news, the huge US corporate media juggernauts were falsely accusing actual journalists of crimes that they themselves have continued to commit on a massive scale, Celente pointed out.

"Fake news? The mainstream media are pros at it. Not a week goes by without a propaganda piece about Syria, Russia, Iran or any of the governments Washington cannot control," Celente observed. The track record of the New York Times and other major US media outlets in putting out fake news unquestioningly on behalf of the US governments of the day went back more than half a century, Celente recalled.

"Fake news? What fake news are they talking about: Saddam Hussein has weapons of mass destruction and ties to al-Qaeda? No, I think maybe the Gulf of Tonkin incident that never happened. How about the propaganda surrounding the shooting down of MH-17?," he noted.

The alleged attack on a US warship in the Gulf of Tonkin in1964 was later proved never to have happened, but reports of it were used to push the US Congress into giving President Lyndon Johnson authorization to respond with what became the Vietnam War. "How about the allegation that US president-elect Donald Trump is [Russian President Vladimir] Putin's puppet and the Russians hacked into Podesta's email?" Celente asked.

© SPUTNIK/ EVGENY BIYATOV Authors of Report on RT & Sputnik 'Propaganda' Refuse to Talk to 'Propagandists' John Podesta was the head of Hillary Clinton's unsuccessful election campaign whose hacked emails released by WikiLeaks revealed instances of corruption and questionable and unethical behavior on the part of the Clinton team. Under a barrage of criticism for losing what their supporters had assumed was a certain victory, the establishment Democrats have responded since the election by criticizing a multitude of allegedly "fake news" sites which they blame for the election defeat. Outgoing US President Barack Obama jumped on the fake news bandwagon during his visits to Germany and Peru, and claimed that fake news harmed democracy.

COMMENT on above article
Pj Alexander

Tacoma, Washington

When Clinton pursues her final push for the throne by alleging foreign intervention and election fraud in three key states that will give her the electorate college win, she will need to have discredited the news sources that will cry foul, so you can bet part of her coup strategy will be to position powerful surrogates as a voice against naysayers.
She has planned a mighty battle with multiple strategic moving parts and we are now seeing it unfold, for it must be fully performed before Trump is sworn into office.
The trolls will be out in over abundance to support election fraud claims, knock Trump and spread revolt, but they will appear educated, kind and thoughtful this go around.
The media has payed their part in positioning her in fresh faced innocense as the coup builds momentum, Google, Tribune publishing and MSM et al will do it's part by keeping the vetted stories that push her to crooked success high in the news feeds,
Trump was only a Clinton plant after all, wasn't he, and the seismic misteps that have recently sent cracks through the foundation of his base have prepared them to crumble at the coming shock and awe. Said it before and I'll say it again: This plot is highly predictable.
Nov 22, 2016 11:16pm Edited

AUTHOR: Here is a commentary from the editor of the Palm Beach Group, a financial newsletter that is subscription based. He calls into question here the mainstream media's self-appointed role as filter of what is and isn't newsworthy. He also puts this notion of "fake news" in historical perspective, pointing out that this trend isn't anything new.

Fake News? It's All Fake by Bill Bonner, the Palm Beach Group Newsletter, December 23, 2016
Source: **http://palmbeachgroup.com/content/palm-beach-daily/fake-news-its-all-fake/32959/**

In January of this year, the *Empire Herald* reported that a "meth-addled couple" had eaten a homeless man in New York City's Central Park.

Later, *Now8News* reported that a can of cookie dough had "exploded in a woman's vagina"; the woman was alleged to be shoplifting.

This week's big news: Russia's ambassador to Turkey was shot and killed. The assailant looked a lot like a 21st-century version of Gavrilo Princip, who lit the fuse for World War I by assassinating Archduke Franz Ferdinand, heir to the Austro-Hungarian throne, in Bosnia.

By the time it was over, 16 million people were dead...

Barbarous Huns

We are writing a series on things that people think they know but ain't so... popular ideas that are wrong, dumb, or misconstrued... which is practically all of them.

In the press lately, for example, is the idea of "fake news."

Supposedly, there is true news, filtered, approved, and administered by the elite media establishment. And there is fake news, such as the deliberately faked stories about cookie dough and meth-addled couples at the beginning of this *Diary*. And there is also news provided by Russian manipulators who supposedly cost Hillary Clinton the White House.

Separating fake from authentic is what we try to do here at the *Diary*. But we are overwhelmed. Half the news is fake, including many of the biggest stories you get from the major media outlets... and reports of fake news! The other half is just mistaken and/or misleading.

In the run-up to America's entry into World War I, for example, the English cut the cable that gave the U.S. direct access to news from Germany. Henceforth, most of the "news" read by Americans about the war came via England, where it was heavily redacted.

The English spun tall tales of German perfidy and German atrocities—including nuns who had been mass raped and children whose arms had been cruelly cut off by the barbarous Huns. None of it was true.

But it did its work; in 1917, gullible Americans rushed troops to join the war... on the side of the English.

Different Shelves

News is rarely what it pretends to be. It is not a bloodless recitation of indisputable facts, like a list of the temperatures recorded at the North Pole.

Instead, every bit of it is informed and persuaded by a web of ideas, myths, and misconceptions. Otherwise, the news would be meaningless.

Every day, millions... no, billions and zillions... of things happen.

The Roman poet Lucretius, way ahead of his time, described life as particles in random collision... Mr. Jones says something to Mr. Smith... a cold breeze blows across the public parks of Duluth... a bird flies into a window pane in Georgia.

If you really wanted to report what happened, you'd have an infinite amount of material.

Obviously, you couldn't do that. Even if you knew what had happened. So, you apply some artificial standards... some "categorical imperatives," as Kant called them. You try to make sense of the world and its goings on by labeling things and putting them on shelves.

It is one thing for a man on the streets of Lagos, Nigeria, to kill another man in the heat of passion. It is quite another for a man in Ankara to gun down the Russian ambassador.

Both involve passions. Both involve men. Both stories end with a corpse. But the former is not newsworthy. Different shelf.

The media decides. It tells us that whatever Mr. Jones said to Mr. Smith, it is not worth reporting. It leaves the cold breeze story to *The Weather Channel*. As for the poor little bird, who gives a damn?

Purveyors of Puffery

Your editor has been the subject of news stories from time to time (referring to himself, Bill Bonner). Unless the article was pure puffery, intended merely to flatter or entertain, the reporters missed the point or misconstrued the facts in such a way that the reader knew less after he had read the article than before.

In one sad instance, an ex-employee committed suicide, distraught over a personal problem. It happened at a time when one of our groups was being investigated by the SEC. (The case ended up as a legal fascination... complicated, but inconsequential... and later largely repudiated by the courts...)

The ex-employee was in no way associated with the alleged wrongdoing. And the infraction had nothing to do with the SEC's usual beat—front-running or market manipulation. But the reporter couldn't resist: "Suicide at Troubled Baltimore Publisher," read the headline.

The reader was left to conclude that the poor fellow offed himself because he was implicated in a trading scam that had never happened or even been alleged.

In another article in the 1980s, your editor was named as part of a "vast, right-wing conspiracy." He had been the director of the National Taxpayers Union, earnestly trying to fight waste in government.

Later, he had hired a private investigator to look into the curious death of Hillary Clinton's law partner, Vince Foster. And now he was criticizing the Clinton administration! The reporter linked us together with other Clinton critics and provided a common cause that never existed.

And now, *The Washington Post*, owned by Amazon.com founder Jeff Bezos, has accused a number of websites and opinion blogs of purveying fake news, some of it fed to them by Russian agents! Yes, Naked Capitalism, Truthdig, Contra Corner, CounterPunch—websites run by former *Wall Street Journal* editors, former congressmen, former Reagan-era officials... left, right, libertarian—and dozens of others were named.

Several of them republish our comments.

We're proud to be among them...

Reeves' Note: When Bill (Bonner) started his research firm in 1978, he made it a mission to counter "fake news" before the term was even coined... Since then, Bill and his team have exposed and predicted the world's most disruptive events. Today, Bill's firm is the largest underground research network on the planet.

AUTHOR: So if the lengthily considered consensus is that fake news is coming at us in all forms and via all mediums, whether that be mainstream media, social media networks and/or viral emails, then what can we, as citizens and news consumers, do to fortify ourselves against this barrage? Below are excerpts from a commentary followed by a recently-concluded study evaluating not only the pervasiveness of false or misleading news, but its effectiveness in getting its messages across. Some suggestions are offered as to how we, meaning the average, everyday consumer of news, can learn to better sift through the mountain of what amounts to trash talk that we are inundated with daily.

Evaluating Information : The Connerstone of Civic Online Reasoning, by the Stanford History Education Group, published November 22, 2016
https://sheg.stanford.edu/upload/V3LessonPlans/Executive%20Summary%2011.21.16.pdf

For every challenge facing this nation, there are scores of websites pretending to be something they are not. Ordinary people once relied on publishers, editors, and subject matter experts to vet the information they consumed. But on the unregulated Internet, all bets are off.

Michael Lynch, a philosopher who studies technological change, observed that the Internet is "both the world's best factchecker and the world's best bias confirmer often at the same time." Never have we had so much information at our fingertips. Whether this bounty will make us smarter and better informed or more ignorant and narrow-minded will depend on our awareness of this problem and our educational response to it. At present, we worry that democracy is threatened by the ease at which disinformation about civic issues is allowed to spread and flourish.

Researchers "shocked" to find students' *in*ability to differentiate between fake and credible news, *NPR*
Source: http://www.npr.org/sections/thetwo-way/2016/11/23/503129818/study-finds-students-have-dismaying-inability-to-tell-fake-news-from-real

"If the children are the future, the future might be very ill-informed. That's one implication of a new study from Stanford researchers that evaluated students' ability to assess information sources"...

The researchers at Stanford's Graduate School of Education have spent more than a year evaluating how well students across the country can evaluate online sources of information.

Middle school, high school and college students in 12 states were asked to evaluate the information presented in tweets, comments and articles. More than 7,800 student responses were collected. In exercise after exercise, the researchers were "shocked" — their word, not ours — by how many students failed to effectively evaluate the credibility of that information.

**More than 80 percent of middle schoolers believed
that 'sponsored content' was a real news story.**

"Many assume that because young people are fluent in social media they are equally savvy about what they find there," the researchers wrote. "Our work shows the opposite."

The students displayed a "stunning and dismaying consistency" in their responses, the researchers wrote, getting duped again and again. They weren't looking for high-level analysis of data but just a "reasonable bar" of, for instance, telling fake accounts from real ones, activist groups from neutral sources and ads from articles.

Most middle school students can't tell native ads from articles.

The researchers showed hundreds of middle schoolers a Slate home page that included a traditional ad and a "native ad" — a paid story branded as "sponsored content" — as well as Slate articles. Most students could identify the traditional ad, but more than 80 percent of them believed that the "sponsored content" article was a real news story.
"Some students even mentioned that it was sponsored content but still believed that it was a news article," the researchers wrote, suggesting the students don't know what "sponsored content" means.

> **They didn't ask where it came from. They didn't verify it. They simply accepted the picture as fact.**
> Sam Wineburg, lead author of the study

Many high school students couldn't tell a real and fake news source apart on Facebook.

One assessment presented two posts announcing Donald Trump's candidacy for president — one from the actual *Fox News* account, with a blue check mark indicating it was verified, and one from an account that *looked* like *Fox News*.
"Only a quarter of the students recognized and explained the significance of the blue checkmark, a Stanford press release noted. "And over 30 percent of students argued that the fake account was more trustworthy."

Most Stanford students couldn't identify the difference between a mainstream and fringe source.

Less than a third of students thought MoveOn.org has a political agenda that might justify skepticism about its data on gun owners.

The American College of Pediatricians (ACPeds) split from AAP in 2002, over objections to parenting by same-sex couples. ACPeds claims homosexuality is linked to pedophilia. It's classified as a hate group by the Southern Poverty Law Center, which estimates that ACPeds has about 200 members.
In an article in Education Week, Wineburg and his colleague Sarah McGrew explain that they directed Stanford undergrads to articles on both organizations' sites. The students spent up to 10 minutes evaluating them, and were free to click links or Google anything they liked.
"More than half concluded that the article from the American College of Pediatricians ... was 'more reliable,' " the researchers wrote. "Even students who preferred the entry from the American Academy of Pediatrics never uncovered the differences between the two groups."

"The kinds of duties that used to be the responsibility of editors, of librarians now fall on the shoulders of anyone who uses a screen to become informed about the world," Wineburg told NPR. "Ard so the response is not to take away these rights from ordinary citizens but to teach them how to thoughtfully engage in information seeking and evaluating in a cacophonous democracy." – Wineburg & McGrew in *Education Week*

Evaluating Information: The Cornerstone of Civic Online Reasoning November 22, 2016
Study from January 2015 to June 2016
Source: entire study that *NPR* article is based on can be found here
https://sheg.stanford.edu/upload/V3LessonPlans/Executive%20Summary%2011.21.16.pdf

Case In Point - Real or Fake?

Queen Bee Michelle's 22 Staffers
http://www.snopes.com/politics/obama/firstlady.asp

Snopes tags this article as "FALSE" but then goes on to say in the body of their analysis:

So far as the original White House report was accurate, it was fair to say that First Lady Michelle Obama had about 22 staffers working for her, directly or indirectly, at the time (Katie McCormick Lelyveld, Michelle Obama's press secretary, set the figure at 24).

ORIGIN: On 1 July 2009, the White House released their Annual Report to Congress on White House Office Staff, a report listing the names, position titles, and salaries of White House employees. Several days later, columnist Lynn Sweet of the *Chicago Sun-Times* put together a blog post in which she used the White House report to identify 22 staffers working in the Office of First Lady. (Sixteen of the listed names were staffers who had the words "First Lady" in their position titles, five were staffers with the words "Social Office" or "Social Secretary" in their titles, and one was listed as a "Staff Assistant.") Lynn Sweet's list was posted to the Last Crusade web site (and the Canada Free Press web site) with the introductory paragraphs (reproduced above) claiming that First Lady Michelle Obama had hired "an unprecedented number of staffers to cater to her every whim," and variants of that version have circulated via e-mail with the subject line "First Lady Requires More Than Twenty Attendants."

Michelle Obama Has 26 Tax Payer Assistants That Make How Much!, by Lauren Richardson, Truth Uncensored, March 16, 2014
Source: http://truthuncensored.net/michelle-obama-has-26-tax-payer-funded-assistants-that-make-how-much/

Never in the history of the White House has a First Lady spent so much on so many personal assistants, all paid from taxpayer dollars. Hilary Clinton had three (3)!

Michelle has 26, from makeup artist Ingrid Miles and hairstylist Johnny Wright to her "chief of staff" Susan Sher whose salary is $172,200.00! The First Lady does not get paid to serve and she doesn't perform any official duties so why so many assistants – to do what exactly? Sort of makes one think the

White House has been mistaken for the Versailles Court of Marie (let 'em eat cake) Antoinette, doesn't it?

This adds up to a whopping $1,600,700.00 and the amount doesn't include the elite benefit packages granted to the White House staff and their significant others (include same-sex partners). Nor does the figure take into account the salaries for the two additional full-time staff members mentioned by Mrs. Obama's Press Secretary nor the full time hair-dresser and makeup artist assigned to her. A guesstimate of the total salaries for Mrs. Obamas attendants is $1,750,00.00 plus the additional benefits.

From Pulitzer prize winning *Politifact*
Glenn Beck says First Lady Michelle Obama has 43 on her staff while Nancy Reagan had just 3, by Robert Farley, *Politifact*, March 4, 2011
Source: http://www.politifact.com/truth-o-meter/statements/2011/mar/04/glenn-beck/glenn-beck-says-first-lady-michelle-obama-has-43-h/

"Edith Roosevelt hired the first social secretary, Isabelle Hagner," Cordery told us via e-mail. "Ever since 1901, first ladies have had assistance carrying out their duties--duties which are not defined in any job description nor laid out in any part of the Constitution. The first lady's correspondence is massive and her obligations as the 'hostess' of the White House have not decreased over time. Once first ladies took on causes (there were some before Eleanor Roosevelt, but she fundamentally changed Americans' expectations of the first lady) then their need for help increased. Modern first ladies like Lady Bird Johnson, Rosalyn Carter, Betty Ford, Barbara Bush, Hillary Clinton, Laura Bush and Nancy Reagan, have all used many more staff people than three."

… So to summarize, Michelle Obama has a staff of 25, not 43 as Beck claimed.

From *Truth or Fiction* (They call this e-news "Fiction" but then clarify the true points as follows) updated 1/8/16
Source: https://www.truthorfiction.com/queen-bee-michelle-obama-largest-first-lady-staff-fiction/

This email has been circulating since 2009. Back then, the White House released a 29-page long ANNUAL REPORT TO CONGRESS ON WHITE HOUSE OFFICE STAFF.
From the report,which can be viewed here:
Source: https://www.whitehouse.gov/assets/documents/July1Report-Draft12.pdf

TruthorFiction.com confirmed a number of staff members and job titles as they appeared in the report, and their annual salaries, as of July 2009. **Many of these staffers and job titles undoubtedly changed in the years that followed.** Also, another important factor is that the job titles don't indicate if a staffer works directly under the president or the first lady, and the forwarded email assumes (falsely) that all of them are personal attendants to Michelle Obama

Basis for claim the "eRumor" is False:
The museum page, which can be viewed here, says former first lady Hillary Clinton had a staff of 20, in addition to 15 interns and volunteers, which also contradicts claims made in the email about staff size.

Forwarded Email Below: (1st circulated July 2009)

WOW! SHE IS WHAT I CALL "HIGH MAINTENANCE!"
Mary Lincoln was taken to task for purchasing China for the White House during the Civil War.
And Mamie Eisenhower had to shell out the salary for her personal secretary from her husband's salary.
Total Personal Staff members for other first ladies paid by you the taxpayers:
Mamie Eisenhower: 1 — paid for personally out of President's salary.
Jackie Kennedy: 1
Rosaline Carter: 1
Barbara Bush: 1
Hilary Clinton: 3
Laura Bush: 1
Michele Obama: 22

First Lady Requires More Than Twenty Attendants – Recession, Depression, What, Michelle Worry? July 7 2009

"In my own life, in my own small way, I have tried to give back to this country that has given me so much," she said. "See, that's why I left a job at a big law firm for a career in public service," Michelle Obama.
(*editor's note: Why did Michelle Obama give up her license to practice law in 1993?Records at the Attorney Registration and Disciplinary Commission of the Supreme Court of Illinois list her status as "voluntarily inactive and not authorized to practice law." It further states that Michelle's license is "on court ordered inactive status." see scan of court document here http://www.wnd.com/2009/08/105998/)

No, Michelle Obama does not get paid to serve as the First Lady and she doesn't perform any official duties. But this hasn't deterred her from hiring an unprecedented number of staffers to cater to her every whim and to satisfy her every request in the midst of the Great Recession. Just think Mary Lincoln was taken to task for purchasing china for the White House during the Civil War. And Mamie Eisenhower had to shell out the salary for her personal secretary.

How things have changed! If you're one of the tens of millions of Americans facing certain destitution, earning less than subsistence wages stocking the shelves at Wal-Mart or serving up McDonald cheeseburgers, prepare to scream and then come to realize that the benefit package for these servants of Miz Michelle are the same as members of the national security and defense departments and the bill for these assorted lackeys is paid by John Q. Public:

1. $172,200 - Sher, Susan (Chief Of Staff)

2. $140,000 - Frye, Jocelyn C. (Deputy Assistant to the President and Director of Policy And Projects For The First Lady)

3. $113,000 - Rogers, Desiree G. (Special Assistant to the President and White House Social Secretary)

4. $102,000 - Johnston, Camille Y. (Special Assistant to the President and Director of Communications for the First Lady)

5. Winter, Melissa E. (Special Assistant to the President and Deputy Chief Of Staff to the First Lady)

6. $90,000 - Medina, David S. (Deputy Chief Of Staff to the First Lady)

7. $84,000 - Lelyveld, Catherine M. (Director and Press Secretary to the First Lady)

8. $75,000 - Starkey, Frances M. (Director of Scheduling and Advance for the First Lady)

9. $70,000 - Sanders, Trooper (Deputy Director of Policy and Projects for the First Lady)

10. $65,000 - Burnough, Erinn J. (Deputy Director and Deputy Social Secretary)

11. $65,000 - Reinstein, Joseph B. (Deputy Director and Deputy Social Secretary)

12. $62,000 - Goodman, Jennifer R. (Deputy Director of Scheduling and Events Coordinator For The First Lady)

13. $60,000 - Fitts, Alan O. (Deputy Director of Advance and Trip Director for the First Lady)

14. Lewis, Dana M. (Special Assistant and Personal Aide to the First Lady)

15. $52,500 - Mustaphi, Semonti M. (Associate Director and Deputy Press Secretary To The First Lady)

16. $50,000 - Jarvis, Kristen E. (Special Assistant for Scheduling and Traveling Aide To The First Lady)

17. $45,000 - Lechtenberg, Tyler A. (Associate Director of Correspondence For The First Lady)

18. $45,000 - Tubman, Samantha (Deputy Associate Director, Social Office)

19. $40,000 - Boswell, Joseph J. (Executive Assistant to the Chief Of Staff to the First Lady)

20. $36,000 - Armbruster, Sally M. (Staff Assistant to the Social Secretary)

21. $36,000 - Bookey, Natalie (Staff Assistant)

22. $36,000 - Jackson, Deilia A. (Deputy Associate Director of Correspondence for the First Lady)

There has never been anyone in the White House at any time that has created such an army of staffers whose sole duties are the facilitation of the First Lady's social life. One wonders why she needs so much help, at taxpayer expense, when even Hillary, only had three; Jackie Kennedy one; Laura Bush one; and prior to Mamie Eisenhower social help came from the President's own pocket.

Facebook, Google to take fake news seriously, by Jon Swartz, Jessica Guynn and Elizabeth Weise, *USA Today* International Edition, November 17, 2016 page 7A

San Francisco Facebook and Google are getting real about fake news sites. Following an avalanche of criticism about how each company inadvertently highlights fabricated headlines and content, the companies say they are pulling ads on such sites.

The actions are intended to stifle the lifeblood of click-bait sites that flourished during the campaign -advertisements. … 'With 1.8 billion members (Facebook) can't hide from the influence it has,' said Drew Margolin, professor of Communication at Cornell University.

AUTHOR: The only thing to do now is 'wait-and-see' how this growing trend of fake news, coupled with consumers' lessening ability for truth discernment, continues to unfold. But I admit, I tend to agree with the point made above that companies (i.e. Facebook, et al.) whose fiduciary duty is to earn dividends for its investors will find a stealth way to circumvent any draconian editorial dictates that cut down on its ability to monetize content – any content.

Chapter 8

Info Wars

...**supporters at campaign stops were enabled to turn in anger against camera operators just doing their jobs, screaming: "*CNN* sucks! *CNN* sucks! *CNN* sucks!"**

- Ed Pilkington, *The Guardian*

Accomplices or antagonists: how the media handled the Trump phenomenon, Ed Pilkington, *The Guardian,* November 22, 2016
Source: https://www.theguardian.com/us-news/2016/nov/22/journalists-media-election-2016-donald-trump

> **Wallace, Fox News Sunday:** It has really been a campaign about, in the case of Trump, his temperament, his behavior, and in the case of Clinton, her ethics, her honesty. If you believe their campaigns, it's the choice between a creep and a crook.

Accomplices or antagonists: how the media handled the Trump phenomenon, Ed Pilkington, *The Guardian*, November 22, 2016
Source: https://www.theguardian.com/us-news/2016/nov/22/journalists-media-election-2016-donald-trump

Since Trump's victory, another theory has been aired increasingly by right-of-center pundits such as Howard Kurtz of Fox News that flips the argument that the media did too little too late to expose Trump on its head. In this iteration, major outlets did too much, were too eager to go after him. The editor of the *Wall Street Journal*, Gerard Baker, tells CJR (*Columbia Journalism Review*) that "some reporters saw it as their role to stop this man from becoming president, they put themselves in the role of partisans".

It fell to Piers Morgan of *Mail Online,* as it often does, to put the case most stridently: "The *NYT's* ludicrously biased anti-Trump barrage of bile helped him get elected."

"That's ridiculous," ripostes the *Times'* Dean Baquet. "We didn't cover Donald Trump any more aggressively than we covered Hillary Clinton. People forget that we broke the story of Clinton's emails. If both sides think you were tough on them, maybe that means you were fair."

AUTHOR: Here's what introspection from the *NYT* has yielded subsequent to the 2016 election:

Lies in guise of news, by Nicholas Kristof, *NY Times* International Edition, Monday November 14, 2016

"If you get your news from this newspaper or our rival mainstream news sources, there's probably a lot you don't know. You may not realize that our Kenyan-born Muslim president was plotting to serve a third term as our illegitimate president, by allowing Hillary Clinton to win and then indicting her; Pope Francis' endorsement of Donald Trump helped avert election-rigging. You perhaps didn't know that Clinton is a Satan worshiper at the center of 'an international child enslavement and sex ring.' Or that Chelsea Clinton isn't Bill Clinton's daughter but a love child of Hillary's by another man – or that Bill has his own love child with a black prostitute.

Oh, the scoops we miss here at *The Times*!

None of those items is actually true, of course, but all have been reported by alt-right or fake news websites (the line between them is sometimes blurred). And one takeaway from this astonishing presidential election is that fake news is gaining ground, empowering nuts and undermining our democracy.

As I've argued for most of this year, I think we in the mainstream media – especially cable television – sometimes bungled coverage of Trump....

A *Buzzfeed* investigation found that of the Facbook posts it examined from three major right-wing websites, 38 percent were either false or a mixture of truth and falsehood. More discouraging, it was the lies that readers were particularly eager to share and thus profitable to publish. *Freedom Daily* had the most inaccurate Facebook page reviewed, and also produced the right-wing content most likely to go viral.

Some of these people promoting these sites aren't even conservatives; they're foreign entrepreneurs trying to build websites that gain a large audience and thus advertising dollars. Alt-right and fake news sites for some reason have emerged in particular in Macedonia, in the former Yugoslavia. *BuzzFeed* found more than 100 sites about U.S. Politics from a single town, Veles, population 45,000 in Macedonia. 'I started the site for a(sic) easy way to make money,' a 17 yr. old who runs *DailyNewsPolitics* told *BuzzFeed*.

Facebook has been a powerful platform to disseminate these lies. If people see many articles on their Facebook feed, shared by numerous conservative friends, all indicating that Hillary Clinton is about to be indicted for crimes she committed, they may believe it.

AUTHOR: Are these info wars and the "rise of Fake News" a recent phenomenon dating from the lead-up to the 2016 U.S. presidential election cycle? Or is this a trend that has been going on, albeit more cleverly camouflaged, for some time now?

To view this phenomena from another angle, let's have a look at what Professor Roger Pielke Jr. from the University of Colorado Boulder had to say recently in his *Wall Street Journal* Op-Ed from December 5th, 2016:

My Unhappy Life as a Climate Heretic, by Roger Pielke, Jr., *Wall Street Journal* European Edition, December 5, 2016

"Much to my surprise, I showed up in the WikiLeaks releases before November's U.S. Presidential election. In a 2014 email, a staffer at the Center for American Progress, founded by John Podesta in 2003, took credit for a campaign to have me eliminated as a writer for Nate Silver's *FiveThirtyEight* website. In the email, the editor of the think-tank's climate blog bragged to one of its billionaire donors, Tom Steyer: 'I think it's fair (to) say that, without Climate Progress, Pielke would still be writing on climate change for 538.'

… I understand why Mr. Podesta – most recently Hillary Clinton's campaign chairman – wanted to drive me out of the climate-change discussion. When substantively countering an academic's research proves difficult, other techniques are needed to banish it. That's how politics sometimes works, and professors need to understand this if we want to participate in that arena.

More troubling is the degree to which journalists and other academics joined the campaign against me. What sort of responsibility to scientists and the media have to defend the ability to share research, on any subject, that might be inconvenient to political interests – even our own?

I believe climate change is real and that human emissions of greenhouse gases risk justifying action, including a carbon tax. But my research led me to a conclusion that many climate campaigners find unacceptable: There is scant evidence to indicate that hurricanes, floods, tornadoes or drought have become more frequent or intense in the U.S. or globally. In fact we are in an era of good fortune when it comes to extreme weather. This is a topic I've studied and published on as much as anyone over two decades.

My conclusion might be wrong, but I think I've earned the right to share this research without risk to my career.

...Instead my research was under constant attack for years by activists, journalists and politicians... For a time I called out politicians and reporters who went beyond what science can support, but some journalists won't hear of this. In 2011 and 2012, I pointed out on my blog and social media that the lead climate reporter at the *NYT*, Justin Gillis, had mischaracterized the relationship of climate change and food shortages, and the relationship of climate change and disasters. His reporting wasn't consistent with most experts' views, or the evidence. In response he promptly blocked me from his Twitter feed. Other reporters did the same.

In August this year on Twitter, I criticized the poor reporting on the website Mashable about a supposed coming hurricane apocalypse... The publication's lead science editor, Andrew Freedman, helpfully explained via Twitter that this sort of behavior 'is why you're on many reporters' do not call lists despite your expertise.'...

...Yet more is going on here than thin-skinned reporters responding petulantly to a vocal professor. In 2015 I was quoted in the *Los Angeles Times* by Pullitzer Prize-winning reporter Paige St. John, making the rather obvious point that politicians use the weather-of-the-moment to make the case for action on climate change, even if the scientific basis is thin or contested.

Ms. St. John was pilloried by her peers in the media. Shortly thereafter, she emailed me what she had learned: 'You should come with a warning label: Quoting Roger Pielke will bring a hailstorm down on your work from the *London Guardian, Mother Jones*, and *Media Matters.*"...

… Yet the climate thought police still weren't done. In 2013 committees in the House and Senate invited me to several hearings to summarize the science on disasters and climate change... In 2014, not long after I appeared before Congress, President Obama's science adviser, John Holden, testified before the same Senate Environment and Public Works Committee. … Mr. Holden responded with the all-too-common approach of attacking the messenger, telling the senators incorrectly that my views were 'not respresentative of the mainstream scientific opinion.' … When the White House puts a target on your back, people notice.

… But the damage to my reputation had been done, and perhaps that was the point.

… Academics and the media in particular should support viewpoint diversity instead of serving as the handmaidens of political expediency by trying to exclude voices or damage reputations and careers. If academics and the media won't support open debate, who will?

AUTHOR: The above passage written by a scientist and academic brings to mind this famous Edward R. Murrow quote: "We must not confuse dissent with disloyalty. When the loyal opposition dies, I think the soul of America dies with it."
According to *Breitbart* and *Fox News*, Newt Gingrich says this fake news reporting has been going on for much longer than many suspect or would care to admit...

Gingrich: NY Times Guilty of 'Totally Fake,' 'Conspiratorial BS' Stories by Pam Key, December 11, 2016
Source: http://www.breitbart.com/video/2016/12/11/gingrich-nyt-times-guilty-of-totally-fake-conspiratorial-bs-stories/

Sunday on *Fox News* Channel's "MediaBuzz," while discussing the fake news controversy, former Speaker of the House Newt Gingrich said of the *New York Times*, "I think if you look back through their coverage of the Trump campaign and the Clinton campaign — to use your language and not mine —they had a fair amount of conspiratorial BS."

He continued, "Things that they would cover that just weren't true. The best example was the woman who repudiated the entire article and said that they took what was a totally positive pro-Trump—'He was a nice man I enjoyed the date.'—and they turned it into Trump hitting on me, acting inappropriately. And she's the one who held the press conference and said this is crazy.
But I'll give you a a much deeper more serious example. Their coverage of Fidel Castro was totally fake. Their coverage of Stalin in the '30s was totally fake."

AUTHOR:
First Blogging (2008), Then Tweeting (2016) Your Way To the Presidency – The first two decades of the new millennia have borne witness to digital age savvy presidential campaigns. When BO's campaign supporters to get him elected took to Facebook to spread the word, they were seen as young progressives working for "hope and change." With the might, both financial and political, that was thrown behind the *Huffington Post* early on by the Liberal-Democrat (and Soros-funded) machine, this assured an unfiltered platform from which to spew their campaign messages and mostly un-factchecked stances on issues and events drawing mainstream media focus during that election cycle.

Fast forward to 2016 and we see a new, emerging pattern on the right in what became labeled as the alt-right. Alt-right, a label now used to refer to a lot of erroneous "-ists" and "-isms", are mostly simply conservatives fed up with the Republican establishment, i.e. DC based lobbyists and politicians – and yet still thoroughly and staunchly conservative. This pattern took shape, in terms of media, in the rise of Breitbart.com, and to lesser extents Newsmax and Fox and also strategically-targeted economy-focused newsletters such as the ones published by the Palm Beach Group. But because Fox was still widely accepted as the dominant conservative mouthpiece when it came to mainstream media and conservative viewership, the candidate who emerged as the front-runner, now our President Trump, jetted past all of them and simply communicated via Twitter.

The real phenomenon is not that he took to Twitter to message his campaign supporters, unfiltered. But that it worked. People paid attention. And Trump's hugely successful one-man presidential communications campaign carried out via Twitter enjoyed this resonance not just with his supporters, but also with mainstream media. It was almost as if editorial offices around the nation, from the *LA Times* to the *SF Chronicle* and *Seattle Post-Intelligencer*, to the *Chicago Tribune* to *Washington Post* to *HuffPost* to the *NY Times*, not to mention the *Wall Street Journal*, *Fox*, *Newsmax* and *Breitbart* had simply one daily directive when it came to coverage of the Trump campaign – all the Tweets that are fit to print. And that turned out to be all of them.

The Rise of The Digital Media Bully Pulpit

Since the rise and prevalence of digital media ca. 2005 the impact it has had on our U.S. Presidential election cycles is immeasurable. Or in another sense, exceedingly measurable, if you credit this new media landscape with helping to elect our last two presidents.

In late 2005, arguably in preparation for the 2008 U.S. Presidential elections, a little blog by the name of *The Huffington Post* was started by an LA-based, millionaire oil-tycoon divorcée and non-profit radio show personality, Ms. Huffington, and a partner, Mr. Ari Emmanuel, brother to the man. Rahm, who would later become Chief of Staff to President Obama once he took the White House.

By 2007, at the Tech Conference held in Orange County, California where Vint Cerf, "father of the internet" spoke and where Twitter was first publicly unveiled to the select crowd of tech executives, tech start-ups and journalists, it had already become the cool kid on the block in terms of that coveted "disruptive technology" status. It was hailed, along with Ms. Huffington, as the news blog that would turn establishment media on its head and usurp mainstream media's dignified mantle of the news source trusted most by the American public and readers around the globe.

And do just that it did. For awhile, at least.

The blog's coronation came during the famous Reverend Wright's "God damn America" tirade. The establishment media reported the frequenting by the Obamas of this Reverend's church throughout decades of their residency in Illinois. Reverend Jeremiah Wright officiated at Barack's wedding to Michelle and baptised both their children. The title of Barack Obama's memoir, *The Audacity of Hope*, was inspired by a sermon given by Reverend Wright. And themes for Obama's 2004 keynote address for the 2004 Democratic National Convention were also taken from sermons given by Reverend Wright. In 2007 Reverend Wright was appointed to Obama's African American Religious Leadership Committee.

The establishment media further proved that the Obamas supported this preacher's sentiment of an America worthy of derision and disrespect to the extent that they continued to attend church services where Rev. Wright screamed God damn America! from his supposedly hallowed bully preacher pulpit.

After the March 2008 media-blitzed scandal broke, for his rebuttal, then-Presidential candidate Obama turned not to the *NYT, Washington Post* or *WSJ* to have his say on the matter but to *The Huffington Post*. Why? Because he knew that they would publish exactly what he told them to publish. In effect, the *Huffington Post* served as the presidential candidate's national megaphone.

And in the elite circles where the media elites think it most matters, namely Los Angeles, NYC, Silicon Valley/ SF, Miami and Chicago, this little blog was being made out to be on a par with the *New York Times, The Washington Post* and *WSJ*. No matter that at the time it was staffed with interns and unpaid writers, called "citizen journalists" back then. And no matter that fact-checking was non-existent at this little blog turned presidential candidate's megaphone. Who cared about fact-checking anymore anyway? And besides, hadn't anyone noticed that the *Huffington Post* trafficked in opinion, glorified Op-ed pieces, not reported facts?

A few months later when this man was elected our 44th president of the United States, it became the scoop of a lifetime. It was now the *Huffington Post* that enjoyed a hallowed bully pulpit. Ordained by the President of the United States, "POTUS," as he now preferred to be called.

The Presidential Candidate Who Tweeted His Way To The Presidency

In this world where technology moves at the speed of light, it's no wonder that, fast-forward to the 2016 presidential election cycle and we were now, once again, in a whole new media landscape. One of the presidential candidates, the "outsider," made headlines from the beginning for his less than amiable relationship with corporate media, "lamestream media" as his like-minded pal, Sarah Palin, liked to call it.

This posture, along with statements he regularly makes at his public political gatherings, won him billions of dollars in "free" corporate media coverage. One analysis has calculated that Trump enjoyed $4.6 billion (according to CNBC.com) in "free" media coverage leading up to his election as the 45th president of the United States.

What's imperative to note is that this Republican candidate's dismay at corporate media was not confined to the liberal-leaning *MSNBC, ABC, CBS, Bloomberg* and *CNN*. But also extended to *Fox*, the lone conservative corporate/mainstream TV news media outlet. So where was a presidential candidate to turn? Well, he turned to his Twitter account. And when he did, he ushered in – successfully ushered in – the era in which we now find ourselves where our President speaks directly to us, regularly and unfiltered, on important issues in 140 characters or less. In other words, he Tweets. And Trump's tweets made headlines throughout the presidential campaign, directed the campaign's and the nation's discourse, and very effectively bypassed mainstream media.

It is also important to note that during the 8 years of an Obama administration, while the little blog called *Huffington Post* rose to dominance and ultimately was sold to AOL for hundreds of millions of dollars ($315M), another little blog, started by a former partner of the *Huffington Post*, Andrew Breitbart, called *Breitbart News*, was still considered "fringe."

Andrew Breitbart, now deceased (2012, at age 43 from sudden cardiac arrest) started *Breitbart News* in his basement in Brentwood, California in 2007. It was his mission to report on Big Government, Big Business and other monolithic entities including even big, corporate-owned media. It was *Breitbart News* that broke the story of ACORN and its community organizing and voter registration tactics (vote early and vote often) for low-income people (September 2009).

It is worth noting that our great country, the United States of America, which prides itself on the principle of fair and balanced news reporting, boasts a media landscape where conservative news outlets are outnumbered at least 10 to 1. And where in the mainstream media television landscape there is only 1 conservative-leaning news outlet, Fox News. And those figures stand even though this outlet enjoys millions of viewers and subscribers. One must ask oneself why? And what is preventing another conservative-leaning news outlet to take part in or share in this right-leaning audience in a way that allows for a self-sustaining business model?

Even today, at this time of writing, now that Mr. Bannon, the former CEO of *Breitbart News*, has been named by the President-elect as his chief strategist, corporate media consistently refers to *Breitbart* as an "alt-right" media platform. Alt-right, in common parlance today, has come to be liberal media's code words for "racism, bigotry, sexism, anti-semitism and misogyny," labeled as such (by liberals) simply as a way to dismiss a cultural revolution they want no part of. But in fact, what this 2016 presidential election has proved, is that "alt-right" media speaks to half the American population who are fed up with corporate media bla bla and more or less most other things establishment, including Big Government.

In other words, in our media landscape today, if your perspective and opinions don't fall in line with those of the mainstream media bullies who still firmly occupy their hallowed bully pulpits, you will be labeled, marginalized and cast aside as the "fringe element." And that's even when your viewpoints are shared by half the country.

What this recent election of our 45th president proves is that those conservative-leaning sentiments are anything but fringe in our country. They are thoughts, opinions, values, sentiments and concerns shared by half our population of legal American citizens. And I am referring to conservative values, not values of "racism, bigotry, misogyny and sexism" which are labels that allow the liberal-leaning contingent to dismiss this new breed of conservatives out of hand, without actually listening to what conservative-leaning people really have to say.

Delegitimizing Mainstream Liberal Media As A Presidential Candidate Platform

So, whereas in 2008 the then presidential candidate's media strategy was to legitimize an upstart blog into a nationally respected mainstream media outlet that would serve as his own and his supporters' personal megaphone, 2016 saw an altogether different strategy.

Jump forward from 2008's presidential election campaign cycle to 2016's, and the media landscape has changed significantly. But, as the French say, the more things change, the more they stay the same. The upstart blog serving as Obama's personal media pulpit, the *Huffington Post*, had, by then, as noted above, been bought by corporate media giant AOL for an ungodly sum. The rest of corporate media had long since caught up and even surpassed this upstart blog in terms of digital media presence. Now, to say the *New York Times* is to at one and the same time refer to both the print version and the digital version. The same holds true for the establishment, corporate, mainstream media in all its forms: tv, print, radio which all exist simultaneously in digital form online.

The front runner Republican candidate for the 2016 election, namely President Trump, took the tactic of delegitimizing the entire cabal of corporate media – calling it mainstream media that missed the stories and misreported the facts. In this sense he was taking a cue from Palin's stance back in 2008 when she famously called it the "lamestream media."

And oh what a difference a few years make. This time people not only listened but the majority of Americans agreed. And corporate media proved them right again and again... and yet again. Right up until the morning of November 9th when the election results proved a resounding, thumping win for Trump. All the more surprising for corporate media listeners and readers who had been told over and over again, right up until the election was called, that the Democratic candidate, Hillary Clinton, was leading by a solid margin in all the national polls and would be our next President.

Who's crying now?

Not so much a rhetorical question since some of the supporters of the losing candidate staged heated, at places turning to violent, protests of the election results even after the losing democratic candidate conceded the election.

But back to the tweets... For a man who, it is said, does not work on a computer, there was no presidential candidate prior to this one, Donald Trump, who so successfully took communicating to his supporters, and ultimately voters, into his own hands. Never mind playing nice with the corporate media folks or doling out media appearances like personal favors to the loyal courtiers, this candidate took to Twitter to blast out his messages, both those that had been covered in the nightly news and those that hadn't.

By one assessment, Trump's Twitter account became the focus of corporate media newsrooms since they knew that by re-publishing and running with any statement he made on Twitter they would dominate the headlines for that day.

What's fascinating to surmise, then, is that both of our last two elected U.S. Presidents successfully turned the media landscape on its head and crafted not just a media strategy that worked, but created a whole new U.S. media landscape.

For Obama it was by legitimizing an upstart blog into being a power-wielding member of mainstream media (the *Huffington Post*). And with President Trump it was by calling out the consistent inaccuracy of news reporting by corporate "mainstream" media and thus delegitimizing it as a reliable source of information throughout the campaign. Instead, many people simply followed his and his campaign manager's Twitter accounts to get updates on what was happening with their candidate during the election campaign. According to numerous post-election analyses, a majority of voters got their news predominantly from their Facebook and Twitter feeds.

In sum, the 2008 presidential election was remarkable from a media perspective in that it successfully legitimized a little-known, "fringe" media outlet into one of the big boys (HuffPo), now owned by corporate media, that served the sitting president as his go-to media megaphone throughout his presidency. The 2016 presidential election is every bit as remarkable from a media standpoint in that the elected president successfully delegitimized corporate media to the point that people paid less and less attention to what it had to say. The 2016 election results simply underscore the lack of credibility the American public now places in its mainstream media elites and sources.

Now that it has been proven without a doubt that the overwhelming majority of political pundits, news editorial boards and other "political experts" in media got the stats, data, and much of the facts wrong and failed to even come close to accurately gauging the pulse of the American people, this failure will prove to be a nail in the coffin of corporate mainstream media for the time being, at least in terms of the public's faith in it as legitimate sources of news and information.

To shift our focus momentarily away from the 2016 US Presidential election and squarely onto the issue of information wars in western, liberal media today, it's worth closer scrutiny of the White Helmets issue. The White Helmets are a self-described Syrian, grassroots aid and relief organization – funded by over $100million from western, NATO governments including the U.S. They are vociferously campaigning for themselves to be awarded a Nobel Peace Prize. Netflix has released a movie about them. At the same time, a handful of credible investigative journalism sources rightly question their validity as more than a media-manufactured propaganda tool.

It is a complicated issue, thorny, too. It is deserving of closer attention as this issue appears to be an emblematic scenario and construct of the Military-Industrial-Media-Academic Complex (MIMAC). The articles cited in this book's bibliography point the reader in a productive direction. With even the top researchers concluding:

> I do not believe that I know exactly what the whole story and the truth is about the White Helmets. But I know that quite a few things don't feel right.
>
> As a sociologist and peace researcher with four decades of academic and practical experience of global affairs and work in conflict zones, the word spoken by the guard Marcellus in Shakespeare's Hamlet at Kronborg Castle in my native Denmark come to mind: "There is something rotten in the state…" not only in the bombing state of Denmark (that supports the White Helmets) but also in the state of the – free – media coverage of conflicts and wars.

– Jan Oberg, Counterpunch, November 4, 2016

Above citation from:
Just How Gray Are The White Helmets of Syria?, by Jan Oberg, *Counterpunch,* November 4, 2016
Source: http://www.counterpunch.org/2016/11/04/just-how-gray-are-the-white-helmets-of-syria/

*Author Note: Regarding this chapter title, please take a look at the glossary at the end of this book to see references to Alex Jones' conservative-oriented media platform called *Info Wars*.

Chapter 9

Can Talking Heads Become Listening Heads?

"When it comes to arrogance, power and lack of accountability, journalists are probably the only people on the planet who make lawyers look good." - Steven Brill

AUTHOR: In today's America, the climate is one where the person who exerts his/her opinion the most forcefully is seen as the most intelligent and where all other differing or competing opinions are seen to be a challenge posed by intellectual inferiors. Today, intellectual inferiorism, in other words, is defined by the sole criteria as those who don't agree with the most vehemently asserted opinion.

But time and again it is proven that those with intellectually superior levels of reasoning rarely put forth their point of view as an ultimate standard of truth, but rather that the more intelligent a person, usually the more they acknowledge that differing points of view can exist simultaneously.

Hence, the intellectual climate we have endured these past 8 years (some would say these past 16 years) has been one where simple minds have ruled by a means of intellectual thuggery in a world of thought and viewpoint intolerance for anyone – everyone – who disagreed with the dominant viewpoint.

Please note, I am talking about the USA. Not Turkey. Not Iran. Not China. Hence this subservience to intellectual thuggery was somehow achieved through complicit acquiescence. But achieved it most definitely was. This was undeniably proved by our recent presidential election and the opinion-making cartel, aka Mainstream Corporate Media, who failed to listen enough to the competing elements of our great nation's thoughts and arguments for its diverse concerns to even register with them in any significant way.

Below quotes are taken from the *Guardian UK*, excerpted from the Columbia Journalism Review's post-election reporter first-person commentary roundup:

Source: https://www.theguardian.com/us-news/2016/nov/22/journalists-media-election-2016-donald-trump from Original Source: http://www.cjr.org/special_report/trump_media_press_journalists.php

Katherine Mangu-Ward, editor-in-chief of Reason: I think both things can be true: the media definitely f**ked up in this campaign and, also, the self-flagellation is reaching Opus Dei levels of hysteria at this point.

Susan Page, Washington Bureau Chief, USA Today: One thing Donald Trump deserves credit for is that during the primaries, not so much now, he was available. He was more accessible than any leading candidate I've ever covered, and more willing to take questions when he had a bad story, not just a good story.

AUTHOR: Is it really the media's job to hold the president hostage? That is, who is serving who? Since November 9th, the President-Elect Trump has been busy assembling his cabinet, taking meetings and making phone calls. During this time there has been much made of the fact that he has refused to be attended daily by a swarm of press. A huge story broke in corporate media about Trump "dodging" the press pool and going out to dinner one evening with his wife. This dodging came on the heels of his refusal to allow the press pool to accompany him to his meeting with the sitting President at the White House to discuss the transition.

The headline in *Mashable* (**Trump dodges reporters again**) most clearly indicates the media's chilling response to this executive decision by its November 16th headline: How Donald Trump's press steak fake-out sends a scary sign to media. The article goes on to state that this behavior "goes against the norm" of previous presidents. But, note, it does not state that there is any law or abiding statute that requires the President-Elect to be accompanied by a press pool at every outing. It then goes on to explain why this behavior of shirking the press pool is so frightening, Because, "It threatens essential direct media access to the president, foreshadowing future attempts to shut out the unfiltered, independent flow of news Americans depend on in holding their elected leaders accountable."

I would argue that the press pool and the media outlets by whom they are employed are the ones that feel threatened. That the President-Elect effectively speaks to his tens of millions of supporters unfiltered via Twitter, Facebook and Instagram is what is really at issue here. There has never been more direct media access by a constituency to its elected candidate.

What we are really witnessing is the slow death of a sort of priestly class. Meaning, back in the Dark Ages when only a small minority could read and write, the majority of the population relied upon the more learned, nearly always, priestly class in order to effectuate documents of significance like birth, marriage and death certificates. However, once literacy swept through the population, thanks largely to Gutenberg's printing press and Martin Luther's cleverness at putting it to good use, things changed.

I would observe that this is the kind of change we are currently witnessing now, at least as it relates to the role of the White House relative to the presidential press pool and the US mainstream corporate media.

To read the entire article of the above-cited Mashable quote: http://mashable.com/2016/11/16/trump-dodges-reporters-again/#94jLCGKll8qW

And to read more about the social impact and phenomenon of Martin Luther's use of the printing press, you can start here: http://patrickkramer.umwblogs.org/2011/09/29/martin-luther-and-the-printing-press/

The issue of Executive Orders in the Obama Administration

Taking a cue from media observer Michael Wolff's admonition that journalists need be first and foremost, if not solely, stenographers, let's examine the issue of Obama's wild run with Executive Actions.

The way the issue was reported in corporate and other media is a case in point as to how journalists are tasked with not just writing down verbatim what is told them by their interview subjects, but are also expected to offer analysis and contextual understanding on some subjects that may be complicated and difficult to grasp by the general public with just a glance-over, superficial reading.

Here are several excerpts from coverage regarding Obama's predilection for Executive Actions. What becomes apparent on closer examination of the issue is that the argument came down to semantics and word play. Congress became alarmed with the former president's "plentiful" executive orders and his "lack of consulting the legislative branch." Obama's riposte was that he issued no more executive orders than many of his predecessors. His statement that he issued them at a rate "less than the previous 100 years" is factually correct.

But, it plays into the assumption that the majority of the public is uninformed about the difference between Executive Orders and Executive Memoranda. According to Phillip Cooper, presidential scholar, Executive Memoranda are simply "Executive Orders by another name."

Executive Memoranda are Executive Orders by another name

So while Obama's assertion is factually correct, it is not truthful and is a statement that is targeted towards a naive and uninformed general public in order to win an argument based on semantics. And while Congress' assertion takes into account Executive Memoranda when asserting its displeasure with the then-president's unilateral executive actions, that wasn't always spelled out in the reporting on this issue.

It is a prime example that illustrates several key points regarding the responsibility of an informed citizenry for a well-functioning democracy and the role of informed journalists who not only report the facts but also exhibit a depth and breadth of understanding of their subject so as to offer analysis and contextual reasoning.

This is not punditry. It is essential to differentiate here that contextual analysis and sifted reasoning is a far cry from opinion and punditry. Opinions, something we saw a lava-flow of throughout the 2016 presidential election cycle, are all too often based on emotion and deep-seated bias. Opinions are also often based on the fashionable trending thought *de jour*, especially in elite media and intellectual circles.

Whereas factual analysis and contextual reasoning is something altogether different. This example

92

below of Obama's abuse, as many would characterize it, of Executive Actions is prime example of this and the necessity for journalists to do their jobs as stenographers, yes. But also as teachers and presenters of facts from all sides so that ultimately the public can make their own informed – key word here, _informed_ – analyses.

The only way this can happen is for the talking heads – that's to say opinion espousing pundits, "political experts" and so-called journalists – to LISTEN. At least to listen more than they talk. As my grandmother used to say, God gave us two ears but only one mouth.

The other key words from above are: an informed and responsible citizenry.

Many are commenting in today's post-2016 presidential election where fake news and info wars ran rampant throughout the campaigns that it is up to each individual American citizen to be able to distinguish between what is true and what is false. Of course, this is true. No one individual can shoulder the duty of being a responsible citizen for another – after all isn't this what the truth of All Men Are Created Equal hangs upon?

But the reality is that most of us, and I am speaking here from the perspective of an ordinary, working, middle class American citizen, have an overwhelming amount of information thrown at us daily. And most of us just don't have the time to sift through it all and become experts in every subject. In fact, to be an expert in all subjects is nigh impossible.

Hence, I would argue that the role of the journalist, for his/her expert analysis, has never been more important than it is today. But that at one and the same time, the potential to abuse that role has never been greater.

In sum, the question today is does the Columbia School of Journalism – or any school of journalism - teach a class in the art of listening? And if not, why not?

Obama's Legacy, An Abundance of Executive Actions, by Clyde Wayne Crews Jr., _Forbes_, January 10, 2016
Source: http://www.forbes.com/sites/waynecrews/2016/01/10/this-inventory-of-obamas-dozens-of-executive-actions-frames-his-final-state-of-the-union-address/#1381579641bc

Some of what transpires today appears without precedent, as even the _Washington Post_ characterized Obama's unilateral executive action on immigration as one that "flies in the face of congressional intent."

The number of executive orders by every U.S. President, by Amrita Khalid, _The Daily Dot_, June 13 2016 later updated on December 20 2016
Source for below: http://www.dailydot.com/layer8/number-of-executive-orders-per-president/

Republicans argue that Obama's executive orders are too plentiful and try to do too much without the input of the legislative branch. House Republicans even authorized a six-month task force to study the impact of what they believe to be an unprecedented use of executive powers in the Obama administration.

"This threat that the president's going to run the government with an ink pen and executive orders, we've never had a president with that level of audacity and that level of contempt for his own oath of office," Rep. Steve King (R-IA), the task force's chairman, said on CNN.

Hudak says there's nothing unique about the issues Obama takes up with his executive orders. They fall commonly in line with that of previous presidents. But unlike other presidents, none of Obama's actual executive orders have been successfully challenged by the courts.

It's true that at 242 executive orders, Obama has issued fewer executive orders than any two-term president than Ulysses S. Grant. It's important to note that this figure does not include presidential memorandums, which Obama has used to address everything from pay increases to federal employees to sanctions in North Korea.

Obama's Legacy, An Abundance of Executive Actions, by Clyde Wayne Crews Jr., *Forbes*, January 10 2016
Source: Forbes http://www.forbes.com/sites/waynecrews/2016/01/10/this-inventory-of-obamas-dozens-of-executive-actions-frames-his-final-state-of-the-union-address/#1381579641bc

President Barack Obama's final-year aspirations as outlined in an earlier-than-usual State of the Union Address will likely showcase executive action on gun control (watch for the symbolic empty chair), Syrian refugees, closing Guantanamo, global warming and addressing themes like income inequality. … In Obama we have a president willing to push boundaries on social and economic issues when it comes to legislating without Congress, a president who taunts Congress with a "We Can't Wait" web page. …

Washington's *lack* of gridlock (of which the Republican grassroots seems to have had its fill this primary season) propels unbounded spending, Obama's pen and phone and regulation without limit. When 2015 ended, I slapped together my latest "Unconstitutionality Index": Last year Congress passed 87 laws, but agencies unloaded 3,408 rules and regulations, for a multiple of 39.

Full Data Graph on all U.S. Presidential executive orders by numbers.
http://www.presidency.ucsb.edu/data/orders.php

Executive Orders vs. Executive Memoranda

"(Executive memoranda) are executive orders by another name"

-presidential scholar Phillip Cooper

Presidential Executive Orders and Executive Memoranda, from The Competitive Enterprise Institute, *Ten Thousand Commandments* 2016 Chapter 3, May 3, 2016
Source: https://cei.org/10KC/Chapter-3

The pertinent question as far as regulatory burdens are concerned is what these executive orders and memoranda are used for and what they do. Executive actions can liberalize and enhance freedom, such as President Abraham Lincoln's Emancipation Proclamation. Or they can expand governmental power, such as President Harry Truman's failed attempt to seize control of America's steel mills or President Franklin D. Roosevelt's confiscation of the nation's gold.

Whether lengthy or brief, orders and memoranda can have significant impacts for or against liberty.

Obama's Legacy, An Abundance of Executive Actions, by Clyde Wayne Crews, Jr., *Forbes*, January 10, 2016
Source: http://www.forbes.com/sites/waynecrews/2016/01/10/this-inventory-of-obamas-dozens-of-executive-actions-frames-his-final-state-of-the-union-address/#1381579641bc

As of the end of 2015, President Obama had issued 242 executive orders according to the Federal Register office, 29 of them in 2015. The White House press office lists an even greater number that includes some not published in the *Federal Register.*

Despite being the most mentioned in policy debate, executive orders are not (yet) the fountain from which most big decrees issue, rather, presidential memoranda are where the real action is.
USA Today called presidential memoranda "Executive orders by another name" that are "not numbered" and "not indexed," Memoranda may or may not be published, depending on a president's determination of "general applicability and legal effect." That makes it tricky to count them....

...Obama's pace for memoranda tops that of the George Bush years. Bush published 129 memoranda that were published in the *Federal Register* over his entire presidency, while President Obama issued 219 during his first seven years, with another year to go.
Not all memoranda get published in the *Federal Register*; additional ones appear on the Obama White House press office page. The chart shows both tallies.

(President Bill Clinton published just 14 memoranda.[57]) https://cei.org/10KC/Chapter-3
Also graph available at this source showing Memoranda vs. Executive Orders for Obama years

Graph Source: http://www.forbes.com/sites/waynecrews/2016/01/10/this-inventory-of-obamas-dozens-of-executive-actions-frames-his-final-state-of-the-union-address/#1381579641bc

Number of Presidential Memoranda

Year	Federal Register Database	White House Tally
2000	13	
2001	12	
2002	10	
2003	14	
2004	21	
2005	23	
2006	18	
2007	16	
2008	15	

2009	38	68
2010	42	70
2011	19	85
2012	32	85
2013	32	52
2014	25	45
2015	31	71
Total: 361		**476**

(Figures updated at www.tenthousandcommandments.com. Sources: Author search on FederalRegister.gov Advanced Search function; Presidential Documents; White House Press Office.)

Presidential Executive Orders and Executive Memoranda, from The Competitive Enterprise Institute, *Ten Thousand Commandments,* Chapter 3, May 3, 2016
Source: https://cei.org/10KC/Chapter-3

...a considerable amount of executive branch activity is not well measured and merits heightened attention, especially when an administration (referring to Obama Administration) so explicitly emphasizes unilateral action.

We live in an era in which the government— without actually passing a law—increasingly dictates parameters of various economic sectors, including health care, retirement, education, energy production, finance, land and resource management, funding of science and research, and manufacturing. Executive actions and decrees issued in a limited government context have different implications than do those issued in an era of activist government, rendering some of what transpires today without precedent. For example, the Internal Revenue Service granted numerous waivers of the Patient Protection and Affordable Care Act's employer mandate without regard to the statute's language.

Counting rules and regulations, executive orders, memoranda, and other regulatory guidance gets us only so far. These actions need more scrutiny and oversight, because they have become powerful means of working around the constitutional system of legislation made by an elected body.

AUTHOR: A President who would be king. And a Congress impotent to stop him.

Reality Check: How Obama Has Actually Issued More Executive Action Than Any President in Modern History, by Ben Swann, *Truth In Media*, January 26, 2016
Source: **http://truthinmedia.com/reality-check-obama-actually-issued-exec-action-president-modern-history/**

Obama has no regard for the Constitution and that his executive action demonstrates that he acts more like a king than a president ...

the Supreme Court is taking a look at whether his executive action on immigration went too far. It's not just immigration where the president has been issuing large numbers of executive actions, he has also announced dozens cf executive actions on gun laws over the past three years. ...

"The truth is, even with all the actions I've taken this year, I'm issuing executive orders at the lowest rate in more than 100 years. So it's not clear how it is that Republicans didn't seem to mind when Bush took more executive actions than I did," stated Obama.

However, that's not the full story. While Obama has issued fewer executive orders than many other presidents, that's actually a word game.

Obama has made prolific use of memoranda despite his own claims that he's used his executive power less than other presidents.

He signed 33% more presidential memoranda in less than six years than Bush did in eight. He's also issued 45% more than last Democratic President Clinton. When these two forms of directives are taken together, Obama is on track to take more high-level executive actions than any president in seven decades.

So what you need to know is that if it feels like Obama is writing law from the Oval Office far more than his predecessors, he is. Obama actually is writing the most since Harry Truman.

However, the other truth is that executive actions aren't just an Obama presidency issue, they have become an executive issue. One where more and more Americans actually want a president to rule by edict and don't see the value of checks and balances.

That's Reality Check. Let's talk about that on Twitter @BenSwann_

AUTHOR: And it wasn't just gun law and immigration that Obama took his autocratic pen to, but also stem cell research, specifically human embryo stem cell research. Through Executive Order 13505, Obama removed an eight-year President George W. Bush-era ban on federally funded stem cell research.

And this was done in an era when the scientific community moved beyond the necessity of human embryos for stem cell research and had the ability to carry out effective research on stem cells without using human embryos. So why the repeal of Bush's Executive Order?

"In section 1, Obama lifted bans that Bush had previously placed on the National Institutes of Health (NIH), prohibiting taxpayer money from being used to obtain stem cells for research. Obama's executive order states that scientists should be able to receive federal funding to purchase and perform research on human embryonic stem cells (hESC)."

Source for above-cited Exec Order: https://www.whitehouse.gov/the-press-office/removing-barriers-responsible-scientific-research-involving-human-stem-cells

Source for above-cited excerpted quote: **The Embryo Project,** https://embryo.asu.edu/pages/barack-obama-executive-order-13505-november-2008

Fellow Trump Critics Maybe Try a Little Listening, by David Brooks Op-Ed article *NY Times* : http://www.nytimes.com/2016/11/22/opinion/fellow-trump-critics-maybe-try-a-little-listening.html

Finally, surely a little universal humility is in order. Orthodox Republicans spent the last 30 years talking grandly about entrepreneurialism while the social fabric around their core voters disintegrated. Maybe a little government action would have helped?

The Democratic Party is losing badly on the local, state and national levels. If you were a football team you'd be 2-8. Maybe you can do better than responding with the sentiment: Sadly, the country isn't good enough for us.

Those of us in the opinion class have been complaining that Trump voters are post-truth, that they don't have a respect for expertise. Well, the experts created a school system that doesn't produce skilled graduates. The experts designed Obamacare exchanges that are failing. Maybe those of us in the professional class need to win back some credibility the old-fashioned way, with effective reform... **But let's be honest: It wouldn't kill us Trump critics to take a break from our never-ending umbrage to engage in a little listening.**

Chapter 10

Going Forward - In A Democracy With A Broken Fourth Estate, What Role Does Media Take?

Without an unfettered press, without liberty of speech, all the outward forms and structures of free institutions are a sham, a pretense—the sheerest mockery. If the press is not free; if speech is not independent and untrammeled; if the mind is shackled or made impotent through fear, it makes no difference under what form of government you live you are a subject and not a citizen. Republics are not in and of themselves better than other forms of government except in so far as they carry with them and guarantee to the citizen that liberty of thought and action for which they were established.

•William E. Borah, remarks in the Senate (April 19, 1917), *Congressional Record*, vol. 55, p. 837.

Source: https://en.wikiquote.org/wiki/Freedom_of_speech

"Donald Trump's unlikely victory has sounded the death knell for the influence and authority of what he and his supporters scathingly call the "mainstream media."
- Ed Pilkington, *The Guardian*

Trump v the media: did his tactics mortally wound the fourth estate? by Ed Pilkington, *The Guardian,* November 22, 2016
Source: **https://www.theguardian.com/media/2016/nov/22/election-2016-donald-trump-media-coverage**

Nando Vila, vice-president of programming and correspondent, Fusion: People's trust in the media and journalists it is at an all-time low, and that should terrify us. I think when you go around the country and you talk to people about this stuff you just realize that what we're providing for them is not what they are asking for or need. We're just very, very separated from them and that's a problem.

Adam Moss, New York magazine: One of the things we learned from all this is that the media as it used to be thought of is just not that important any more. It didn't matter that some people were doing good work because most places – the *New York Times*, us, the *Washington Post*, Bill Maher, God knows – we're just talking to ourselves and we're talking to people who already agree with us.

Weisberg, the Slate Group: I think that journalists' fundamental responsibility is to tell the truth and describe reality, and journalists are now going to have to do it under this tremendous pressure of normalization: to treat Trump like a normal Republican within the range of our political experience, to take his ideas seriously, to not constantly bring up the outrageous things he's said and done.

Accomplices or antagonists: how the media handled the Trump phenomenon, Ed Pilkington, *The Guardian,* November 22, 2016
Source: **https://www.theguardian.com/us-news/2016/nov/22/journalists-media-election-2016-donald-trump** from original source:
http://www.cjr.org/special_report/trump_media_press_journalists.php

**"From a bonanza of free air time to an overt media campaign against him,
Donald Trump was a candidate covered like no other."**
- Ed Pilkington

AUTHOR: The media's coverage of our 2016 presidential election created an atmosphere where both sides took unceasing potshots at one another, true. But it also opened us up – meaning the United States – to worldwide international criticism, especially on the state of our media establishment, but also even on the state of our political processes. Of course, the irony (below) of a state-run media outlet commenting on the US media establishment's enfeebling of our democratic process is a milestone in our country's history.

It also pulls into focus the point made in the previous chapter that the claim of non-partisan, objective reporting that our Western media makes allows for a more insidious rooting of (self-)censorship than perhaps any state-owned media could ever aspire to. The old tale of the frog placed in warm water that is slowly brought to a boil, comes to mind. The frog in that situation will stay in the water until its life is boiled out of it. Whereas, when a frog is dropped into boiling water, it will jump out, or at least die trying.

China's media casts U.S. As dysfunctional by Chris Buckley, *New York Times* International Edition, December 16, 2016

..."China's ruling elite seems to be consoling itself with the idea that the American president-elect will take charge of a country staggering into decline and disunion. A flow of articles in Communist Party publications in recent weeks has argued that the United States' tumultuous past year showed it to be dysfunctional and dissolute, and blighted by... an enfeebled news media.

..."'Mainstream Chinese views of the United States have shifted from admiration to doubt, especially after the financial crisis, and now increasingly to rejection of its values,' Shi Yinhong, the director of the Center for American Studies at Renmin University in Beijing, said in an interview.
..."' Trump's victory, like 'Brexit,' is seen as an opportunity for the official media to teach the public they have no reason to envy the West.' ....the series excoriated the American news media, including *The New York Times*, for failing to anticipate and explain Mr. Trump's rise, especially among blue-collar voters.

'It's difficult for such a media to reflect the realities of America,' read one commentary in that issue (referring to the *People's Daily*, the chief newspaper of the Communist Party). 'How much it can contribute to the development of American democracy is also doubtful.'

...There is some irony in all this – not least, in a heavily censored party-run paper that faithfully echoes official views scolding the American news media for failing to take on the powerful."

Donald Trump's win means the biased media needs to change, by Michael Goodwin, *NY Post*,
November 13, 2016
Source: http://nypost.com/2016/11/13/donald-trumps-win-means-the-biased-media-to-change/

The election was in part a referendum on the media, and Trump's victory is their earthquake. The remarkable admission by the *New York Times* that it failed to appreciate Trump's appeal is just the start of an overdue shake-out.

As such, it gives the president-elect a perfect opening to fundamentally change White House press relations. A fresh approach would be good for Trump and great for America.

The goal should not be revenge, though Trump can't be blamed for wanting it. Rather, the goal should be to have continuing conversations with Americans so he can understand their concerns and get their reactions to his ideas — without the biased filter of elite news outlets.

Now that everyday Americans have taken back the country, it's time for the old guard media to take a back seat.

The *Times*, as the leader of the liberal wolf pack, launched an unprecedented attack to pick the president. By abandoning fairness, the paper lost its credibility and is hemorrhaging readers and money. Others are likely in the same fix, and broadcast networks were on the wrong side of history.

Trump should seize the chance to end their stranglehold on politics, culture and everything else. The best thing he can do is deny the establishment organizations their key advantage — a monopoly on access to power.

He must shock them out of their entitlement, which has bred contempt for the presidency, the public and honest journalism.

101

For generations, Democratic and Republican presidents kow-towed to the *Times*, the *AP, CBS* and a few others. Any president wanting to make something public had an aide call one of them and say the president plans to do this or that — it's all yours.

Presto, there it was, front page or top of the evening news, the inside scoop on the president's plans. Favored reporters and pundits were summoned for "background" briefings in the Oval Office.

Even the chance to ask the president a question at press conferences was doled out like candy as a reward, or withheld as punishment.

Obama played the game brilliantly because he knew liberals would transcribe his thinking, support him and denounce dissidents. "60 Minutes" was his go-to show, with softball interviews by Steve Kroft expected and delivered.

It is a rotten system of big-boy favoritism, and Trump, who also agreed to a "60 Minutes" sit-down, should instead smash the mold. He can democratize the scoops by boosting the power of smaller organizations.

Most important, he should get closer to the public by taking advantage of the technology to further erode the power of gatekeepers... There are endless opportunities for a new way of connecting the government to its bosses — and the media would have to report on these events without controlling them.

Obama complained about the Washington bubble, but even when he left town, he didn't leave the bubble. He gave speeches to adoring crowds, donors and compliant journalists. There was little listening to unfiltered public concerns.

Trump has a different constituency, and needs to fashion a new way to stay connected to the country. Above all, to keep his promise to be the people's voice, he must first know what the people are thinking. ...

Feeling the spirit of '76 in 2016

With echoes of "Hamilton," reader Denis Ian views Nov. 8, 2016:

"Two dozen decades ago, the British Empire bent a knee and grudgingly offered a sword of surrender to an army of Deplorables led by George Washington.

The embarrassment was so mighty, the commander of the defeated couldn't bear to offer his own sword and delegated the display of humility to an underling, slighting the victor and bruising protocol.

The honors of war also called for a British band to play a song chosen by the victors. Legend has it that Washington requested 'The World Turn'd Upside Down.'

Now the world is again turned upside down. And once more, the underdog outclassed the mighty and, with a legion of Deplorables, pointed to a new and brilliant future.

To bruise the words of Benjamin Franklin, who I am sure is in sweet shock, we have our republic back … IF we can keep it.

This time, we better pay more careful attention. We are ever lucky for this second chance.

We let others hijack our principles, kidnap our values, and hostage our free speech. We permitted a slender few to tell us who we were to be, rather than honor who we are. We let them guilt us into a nightmare from which we have been freed.

AUTHOR: Revolutions, even when won, do not come easily to the victors, nor to the so-called vanquished. If we are willing to accept that our world has been 'turned upside down,' then it stands to reason that there will be winners and losers in this re-organization of the American status-quo.

Whether or not the coming months and years play out as such, the fact that corporations are already responding to the smaller, non-mainstream media outlets by withholding advertising dollars in the wake of the Trump victory, attests to the power structure's willingness to impose a kind of false-market-regulated censorship. As noted in the above chapter, in spite of Rush Limbaugh's huge listenership and reach into potential marketshare, his radio show was pulled from major markets and as an outlet for advertisers leading up to the 2016 presidential election. Hence it would appear that whether media outlets are outright owned by big corporations or not, nearly all must be wary of biting the hard that feeds them. Where we may potentially eventually see a market correction in this equation is when corporations recognize the fact that there are millions of consumers being ignored, and that these consumers no longer pay much, or any, attention to mainstream media.

Advertisers pulling ads from Breitbart, by Shareen Pathak, *Digiday,* November 22, 2016
http://digiday.com/brands/brands-pulling-ads-placed-breitbart/

"Brands and the agencies that work for them are caught in a tough place when it comes to ads on so-called alt-right websites like Breitbart,...
Thanks mostly to programmatic advertising, plenty of brands advertise on Breitbart,...Now, a number of them — including Allstate, Modcloth, Nest, Earthlink and SoFi — are blacklisting the website, under pressure in social media and even blaming the digital ad system for appearing there in the first place. ...

The counter argument to this kind of pressure is the reality that Breitbart attracts a large and loyal audience. According to comScore, the site attracted 19.2 million visitors in October. And after the election, more brands and agencies are recognizing the need to talk to the rest of the country."

Trump v the media: did his tactics mortally wound the fourth estate?, Ed Pilkingdon, *The Guardian*, November 22, 2016
Source: Ed Pilkington https://www.theguardian.com/media/2016/nov/22/election-2016-donald-trump-media-coverage?

"What typically drives TV is great reporting by newspapers. Instead, Trump used his tweets as an alternative route to great journalism, and that turned out to have been a very big deal," Smith told the *Guardian*.

The TV channels feasted on tweeted Trumpisms with an alacrity that many observers found disturbing. (*Author's Note: Smith here refers to Ben Smith, editor-in-chief of *BuzzFeed*)...

A more disturbing thought is that while many news outlets took great efforts to chronicle the plight of the white working classes in middle America, their dispatches didn't register with millions of voters for the simple reason that those voters weren't reading any of us. Amid the ongoing muscle of *Drudge*, the new transcendence of *Breitbart*, not to mention the proliferation of fake news sites, conservative Americans – and for that matter liberals – are increasingly able to receive information from within their own alternative bubble where their opinions are reinforced without being challenged by the loathed MSM.

One of the more despairing expressions of this theory was given by New York magazine's Adam Moss to CJR: "The media as it used to be thought of is just not that important any more. It doesn't matter that some people were doing good work because ... we're just talking to ourselves and people who already agree with us."....

..."This is a moment of high danger for the press; we're heading into a dark period for American democracy and American journalism," says Jay Rosen of NYU. Jorge Ramos tells CJR: "I think we'll remember this election as unique and very concerning for the future of the press because if this becomes the norm, we are in serious trouble." ... There's also the internal danger that the media will normalize his time in office under the cloak of traditional reverence for the presidency.

Amid backlash, Twitter vows to crack down on hate speech, by Jessica Guynn, *USA Today* International Edition, November 7, 2016, Money 7A

"While we have taken steps over the years to try to combat abuse and harassment, we haven't moved as quickly as we would have liked or we haven't always done as much as we would have liked because we have tried to make sure we are not making decisions that have unintended, negative consequences and ramifications," - Del Harvey, Twitter's head of safety.

..."Twitter is making changes to notifications, allowing users to mute words, phrases, emojis, even entire conversations, because, Harvey says, abuse 'is acutely felt in notifications.' Eventually Twitter will expand the mute function to everywhere users see tweets. Twitter already allows users to mute accounts they don't want to see tweets from.

Accomplices or antagonists: how the media handled the Trump phenomenon, Ed Pilkington, *The Guardian,* November 22, 2016
Source: **https://www.theguardian.com/us-news/2016/nov/22/journalists-media-election-2016-donald-trump** from Original Source:
http://www.cjr.org/special_report/trump_media_press_journalists.php (Journalists' quotes cited from the *Columbia Journalism Review's* study referenced in article and prior chapters of this book.)

So what will be the role of the "mainstream media" as it embarks, somewhat battered but still standing, into Trump's America? Will it be to document the new administration with a detached and "objective" eye, as traditional newsroom canons dictate, or will it pursue that other burning function of the fourth estate, holding power to account?

"We will cover him fairly and aggressively, and we will not let his criticism of us sway us or keep us from doing what we have to do," says Dean Baquet of the *New York Times....*

...Social media takes on an increasingly large role in the campaign, as Trump and Clinton use it to circumvent traditional media and journalists mine it for stories. Brutal harassment of journalists on social media becomes the new normal.

Craggs, Slate: Trump identified a weakness in the way online political media, or just online media in general, operates. He won the primary largely by sucking all the oxygen out of the room. In this crowded field his was the only name that people saw out there all the time. People didn't get a chance to know who John Kasich was or what Chris Christie had to say. Trump can command the attention from a country's entire political media by just being an idiot on Twitter at 3am.

Martin, the New York Times: There's no question that part of the Trump story is that institutions in this country do not have the authority and gatekeeping capacity that they used to have. I think everybody recognizes that.

Goldberg, the National Review: One of the reasons [the mainstream media is] in so much trouble right now when it comes to Trump is that they have a huge "cry wolf" problem. It was Daniel Schorr, in 1964, who said Barry Goldwater's trip to Europe after he had secured the nomination was really a clandestine trip to meet up with neo-Nazi elements. They have been doing this for a very long time. So when the press says that every Republican who's nominated, including Mitt Romney of all people, is a monster, and then the Republican party nominates a monster, you guys don't understand why half the country couldn't give a rat's ass. That's on you guys to a considerable extent.

Ramos, Univision and Fusion: I think our social role is to challenge those who are in power and on many occasions the press has failed in doing that. It took Hillary Clinton hundreds of days to have her first press conference, and that is not right, and Donald Trump chooses who covers his press conferences or not. This is completely unprecedented. I think we'll remember this election as unique and very concerning for the future of the press because if [this] becomes the norm, we are in serious trouble.

Mainstream Media's Reputation Currently Broken, by Kathleen Parker, *Newsmax Media*,
November 20, 2016
Source: http://www.newsmax.com/KathleenParker/trump-journalism-political-
media/2016/11/20/id/759851/

Of all the losers in this season of discontent, the mainstream media top the list. I don't say this lightly
and sincerely fear that loss of faith in journalism ultimately will cause more harm to the nation than any
outside enemy could hope to.

Only 18 percent of Americans trust national news and just 22 percent trust local news, according to the
Pew Research Center. That said, three-fourths of Americans think news organizations keep political
leaders in line, though about the same percentage think the news media are biased.

Not surprisingly, Republicans more than Democrats think this way. It hasn't helped that Republican
politicos and conservative cable and radio outlets have convinced their constituents that the media are
the enemy. It seems we've forgotten that the purpose of a newspaper, as *Chicago Evening Post*
journalist and humorist Finley Peter Dunne put it in an 1893 column, is to comfort the afflicted and
afflict the comfortable.

Could there be a better reason to give Donald J. Trump a rough ride?

Nevertheless, distrust of legitimate journalism is no joking matter. What happens to democracy when
an uninformed, misinformed, or dis-informed populace tries to make sound decisions? The simple and
terrible answer is, democracy fails.

We've reached this critical juncture thanks largely to the digital revolution....

Also contributing to the growing distrust is the perceived blurring of news and opinion, which can be a
legitimate beef. Advocacy journalism, in this opinion writer's view, belongs on the editorial and op-ed
pages, though many news organizations subscribe to the notion that advancing a social cause or,
perhaps, derailing an unfit candidate, justifies aggressive, Page 1 coverage. Objectivity be damned. ...

...Fortunately, only 4 percent of Americans trust social media "a lot" as a news source, and 30 percent
trust it "some," according to Pew. But sometimes it's hard to tell fake from true, or advocacy from
propaganda, and therein lies perhaps the greatest challenge of our time.

What's clear is that news consumers must be extra vigilant in selecting news sources, while also being
self-critical about those choices. The mainstream media need to work harder at presenting balanced
reporting to rebuild trust. And education programs aimed at teaching students how to evaluate news,
such as those created by The News Literacy Project, need greater public support and an accelerated
timeline.

Zuckerberg and Facebook must defend truth, By Jim Rutenberg, *International New York Times*, November 22, 2016

"Truth doesn't need arbiters. It needs defenders. And it needs them now more than ever, as the American democracy staggers into its next uncertain phase.

With a mainstream news media that works hard to separate fact from fiction under economic and political threat, Facebook – which has contributed to that economic threat by gobbling up so much of the online advertising market – is going to have a special responsibility to do its part.

Just imagine what things will look like if the unsavory elements that tore through the 2016 election – false narratives, fake news and aggressive efforts to delegitimize traditional journalism – come back into play as Donald J. Trump presses to enact his agenda....

AUTHOR: Interesting how this *New York Times* Business page writer clarifies the "economic threat" in his above commentary but fails to clarify the "political threat." That this was written while the Obama administration was still in office and was winding up its 8 years of White House occupation, it would be enlightening if Rutenberg had clarified just what he meant by his statement "mainstream media...under political threat." Fill us in, won't you please? Meaning, in your own words.

AUTHOR: Advertising $$ are now attempting to be used to determine which media can and cannot exist, which voices, ultimately will be heard and which voices will be silenced.

Breitbart declares war on Kellogg's after brand pulls advertising, by Shareen Pathak November 30, 2016
Source: http://digiday.com/brands/breitbart-calls-boycott-kelloggs-brand-pulls-advertising/

Ad tech firm AppNexus also has barred Breitbart News for hate speech.

Political pressure on brands has reached new highs in an unprecedentedly charged climate: New Balance was threatened with a boycott from liberal customers for showing support for Trump's stance on trade; Chobani's CEO has come under fire by the far right for being an outspoken critic of Trump's. *Breitbart*, in the post urging its readers to boycott Kellogg's, said that the brand offered no examples of how its readers don't align with the brand's values. It included a list of Kellogg's brands in the post...

The site, which says it receives 45 million monthly readers (comScore estimates it attracted 19.2 million readers in October), said that Kellogg's decision to drop the site from its rotation of advertising represents an "escalation in the war by leftist companies ... against conservative customers whose values propelled Donald Trump into the White House."

The site is also posting news articles alongside the boycott post saying that Kellogg's is complicit in child labor abuses, citing an Amnesty International report on companies that use palm oil made on plantations overseas.

AUTHOR: Clearly, for a strong, independent media to exist and for it to have a foundation from which to act as the fourth estate, a new – successful – business model must be achieved. Below is perhaps a future model? The platform mentioned below, Patreon, is a sort of crowdfunding for media projects platform.

The Rubin Report, A talk show about big ideas and free speech. Hosted by Dave Rubin.
http://www.rubinreport.com/about#crew
Hosted on the platform: https://www.patreon.com/rubinreport

"Dave is passionate about reinventing the way current events are talked about. No paid pundits, no partisan hacks, no screaming lunatics. Just real people having real conversations about the hottest issues of the day. "

AUTHOR: The *NYT* has been quick to not only spot but also capitalize on the financial opportunity in all of this. This next excerpt was taking from a speech by Mark Thompson of the *NYT* first delivered at the Detroit Economic Club in mid-December 2016. The British-born former BBC News producer Mark Thompson became the president and Chief Executive Officer of the *New York Times* in 2012.

In a world of fake news, real journalism must be paid for, by Mark Thompson, *The Guardian*
Media Opinion, December 16 2016
Source: https://www.theguardian.com/commentisfree/2016/dec/16/fake-news-journalism-digital?
CMP=share_btn_link

What about publishers? Well, we're not perfect either. Professional news organisations like the *New York Times*, where I'm the president and chief executive officer, screw up from time to time and we have to learn from our mistakes.

But at least the user of the *Times* or the *Guardian* enjoys complete transparency when it comes to accountability. You can see who wrote the story and, if you think it's inaccurate or biased, you know who the editor is, and the publisher. The ultimate provenance of content, and the algorithms that decide what we see and don't see, lack this clarity.

What professional news organisations should stand for, now more than ever, is tough-minded, independent journalism edited and delivered without fear or favour. At the *New York Times*, we want every story we report, every column of opinion we publish, to be worth paying for.

And, to state the obvious, we believe in the opposite of fake news. We want people here and around the world to have access every day to real news, to form their own judgment about what is happening in their world.

Real journalism is vital to our democracy, and it has to be paid for.

If not, it will largely disappear and leave the field open for Pizzagate, and Trump's zombie army of illegal voters.

If you as a citizen are worried about fake news, put your money where your mouth is and pay for the real thing.

*This is an edited version of a speech Mark Thompson delivered at the Detroit Economic Club earlier this week (as of December 16, 2016)

AUTHOR: Following a few days on the heels of this speech, loyal employee, Jim Rutenberg, seconded this appeal for paid subscribers by echoing this same "fake news" threat in the following article:

Trump's attacks on the press may save it, by Jim Rutenberg, *The New York Times* International Edition, Tuesday December 20, 2016, page 10

… "But Mr. Carter (Graydon Carter, ed. of *Vanity Fair*) seized the moment with a red banner on the home page calling Vanity Fair 'The Magazine Donald Trump Doesn't Want You to Read," and imploring visitors, "Subscribe Now!"

Lo and behold, subscriptions spiked a hundredfold over their daily average, the magazine said, bringing *Vanity Fair's* parent company, Condé Nast, the biggest number of new daily sign-ups in its 116-year history. …

As Mr. Trump tries to burn the media village down, he may be saving it.

His running campaign of Twitter attacks, declarations of failure and vows to punish the news media is threatening to do what so many years of cost-cutting and re-envisioning could not do as easily: put the industry on more solid economic footing, where customers who realize its value are willing to pay for it more regularly.

It's early. And, in traditional media, hope is the province of masochists. But in the weeks since the election, magazines like T*he New Yorker, The Atlantic* and *Vanity Fair*; newspapers including the *New York Times, The Wall Street Journal, The Los Angeles Times* and *The Washington Post*; and nonprofits like *NPR* and *ProPublica* have been reporting big boosts in subscription rates or donations.

It's as if Mr. Trump's media attacks have combined with the heightened attention on the perils of fake news to create one big fat advertisement for the value of basic journalism. …

...Real reporting costs real money. But newsrooms, saddled with big losses in advertising, are continuing to contract. ...That's where the new subscriptions come in. If they keep growing – sure, a big if – they could bring what *The Los Angeles Times's* editor in chief and publisher, Davan Maharaj, called "a new golden era in journalism."

AUTHOR: When I started out in journalism in the early 90's, the publishing and editorial branches of respected newspapers, magazines and other news media were always separate. There was no crossing the line. It is significant to note in the above commentary by the NYT's Rutenberg that he apparently doesn't even blink an eye when describing the head honcho's title at *The Los Angeles Times:* publisher *and* editor in chief. Meaning, the same person who pockets the advertising bucks decides what stories get published and how. Am I the only one who sees a conflict of interest here? Since when have those lines been so blithely blurred?

Another thing to underscore is that *Vanity Fair* and *The New Yorker,* along with *Wired, Vogue, GQ,* et al. are all Condé Nast publications, meaning owned by the same corporation. Interesting in July 2016, Conde Nast, operating out of their new One World Trade Center headquarters, announced the launch of Condé Nast Spire, a new division that focuses on finding links between consumers' purchasing activity and their content consumption by connecting the company's own collected user data, i.e. its own 'first-party behavioral data.' Advance Publications is the parent company of Condé Nast. To see a complete listing of their holdings, refer to this link on the Columbia Journalism Review. http://www.cjr.org/resources/?c=advance Advance Publications is a multi-billion dollar privately-held corporation that also owns Parade Publications, Inc., and Random House, Inc. It is the country's largest privately-held newspaper chain. To read more, see *Forbes'* article, **These Fifteen Billionaires Own America's News Media Companies**. http://www.forbes.com/sites/katevinton/2016/06/01/these-15-billionaires-own-americas-news-media-companies/#4232f2f330b4

AUTHOR: There is nothing new nor innovative about this kind of response to a crisis in journalism and media. For precedent we can look to I.F. Stone's Weekly (I.F. Stone, Isadora Feinstein Stone, b. 1907, d. 1989) which he began as a paid weekly mailer back in 1952. He did this as a response to *PM, The Star* and the *Daily Compass* closing that winter.

We can read from his dedicated website about the success of this early initiative to counter big media.

I.F. Stone's Weekly, The Website of I.F. Stone, Source: http://www.ifstone.org/weekly.php

When *PM, The Star* and the *Daily Compass* had closed in the winter of 1952, I.F. Stone decided to start "I.F. Stone's Weekly" by soliciting the mailing list of The Daily Compass using direct mail. This was not as simple as it sounds today. Letters had to be stuffed by hand and sorted; after some had been mailed, it turned out that the printed material had omitted the subscription price ($5.00) although $10.00 had been correctly mentioned for air mail. Somehow, by mailing 30,000 readers and running some ads, 5,200 charter subscribers were secured. This list grew to 20,000 by 1963 and 70,000 in its final year, 1971.

Postage costs were extremely low because the *Weekly* went out second class for 1/8 of a cent per copy or about 6 cents per year per reader. This Government postal subsidy made it possible for the Weekly to be published and distributed for a $5 subscription price that never changed. But because I.F. Stone and Esther Stone ran the Weekly together as an economical "mom and pop" operation, it was in the black from the beginning.

By the time it closed, with 70,000 readers, it was grossing $350,000 per year or, in year 2007 dollars, perhaps over $2,000,000 per year.

AUTHOR: More recently there has been the emergence of micro news sites such as *The Intercept* where Glenn Greenwald is co-founder. Greenwald was awarded the Pulitzer Prize for public service in 2014 for his NSA reporting he did while at *The Guardian*. Note that the documentary film about Edward Snowden, Citizenfour, that Greenwald collaborated on as a writer and journalist, was the recipient of an Oscar (Best Documentary) at the 2015 Academy Awards. For some that alone spells a measure of collusion with the establishment, for others it's a symbol of achievement. Greenwald is also a constitutional lawyer as well as *NYT* best-selling author. One of his books, *No Place to Hide,* is about the U.S. Surveillance State.

This below cited article is from a micro news site/blog, one that has seen very little funding, which is the case in the majority of micro blogs. *The Intercept,* on the other hand, noted above, is extremely well-funded. Its parent company is First Look Media. This is how they describe themselves: " First Look Media is a new-model media company devoted to supporting independent voices across all platforms, from fearless investigative journalism and documentary filmmaking to smart, provocative entertainment. Launched in 2013 by eBay founder and philanthropist Pierre Omidyar, First Look operates as both a studio and digital media company. Entertainment with something on its mind." (Source for quote: *https://firstlook.media/jobs/*)

The Audacity of An Arrogant Despot, A Micro-blog - *Sword At the Ready,* September 2011
Source: https://swordattheready.wordpress.com/2011/09/01/the-audacity-of-an-arrogant-despot/

"Obama calls for a joint session of Congress to give a campaign speech about jobs – on the same night and time as the Republican Presidential Debate"
White House Press Secretary Tells GOP "They can reschedule".
UPDATE: Speaker John Boehner refuses to convene the session, asks Obama to choose another night.
By INVAR

It's just incredible. As far back as this blog's inception, warnings about the arrogant condescension of His Heinous, Barrack Hussein Obama doesn't assuage the incredulity that his regime generates. It's truly surprising.

What is stunning, is not the hubris itself that was expected from this President, but the acceptance of it by large majority of Americans whom historically, have rejected such blatant arrogance from it's civil servants.

It's amazing to watch and hear the blatant and in-your-face efforts this regime is ramping up, taunting and almost daring someone to defy him. There's not even a semblance of courtesy or gentlemanly statesmanship from this regime. The monarchy of Louis the XVI's cannot compare to the extravagance and disdain this Administration showcases.

Because the collapsing economy and the need to create jobs are so important to The One, he decided that he would wait until AFTER his ninth vacation and 68th round of golf since he was crowned in 2009 to give what the media will most likely dub 'his most important speech as President' to outline his own "jobs" plan. We assume His Heinous will entreat the country with yet another demand for a trillion-dollar "stimulus" designed to grow the government behemoth even larger and bankrupt the nation further into eternal debt.

But given that we know Obama is a broken teleprompter of useless campaign tripe and class warfare, what was startling about Obama's call for a joint session of Congress to deliver another lecture in Socialism, is the day and time he demanded it.

111

You see Wednesday September 7th at 8 PM Eastern, is the Republican Debate from the Reagan Library. A date that was planned and set since May 3, 2011 at 4:59 PM.

But the audacity of Obama knows no bounds, and in typical Chicago Political Thug fashion – he decides to try and nullify the Republican event altogether by holding the networks captive to cover a joint session of Congress for the purpose of providing a platform for another Obama teleprompter speech. And speaking of joint sessions of Congress, those are given historically for special occasions like the State of the Union or urgent situations such as declarations of war or consultation for use of force authorizations. To use such occasions to attempt to ramrod yet another big government political agenda down the nation's throats is again, the audacity that characterizes the Obama regime.

Where the arrogant condescension and disdain are self-evident, is in the remarks by Obama's Propagandist in Chief: Jay Carney.

First he lies and says that the scheduling of the request at the same time and date as the GOP Debate is 'coincidence'. Obama sent the request for the joint session on Wednesday, the Debate has been set since last May. Does Carney really think the American people are stupid enough to assume that the Obama regime did not know when the Republican debate was going to occur?

But I'm more interested in the choice of words and tone this guy used.

> "It is one debate of many [that will air] on one channel of many… [and] there are many other factors here" to consider when scheduling a major address from the president….Carney gave NBC his permission to reschedule the Republican debate so it doesn't conflict with the president's speech, saying "if the network so chose and the candidates so chose" to reschedule, "that would be completely fine with us."

How mighty white and benevolent of him to grant 'permission' for a news network to reschedule an event they had set since May to accommodate an egomaniacal narcissist who can't get enough of his face on TV to lecture the American people and make demands!

But miracles do sometimes happen, and the Speaker replied to the request from the White House with these words:

> "Sept. 8th would be better "so we can ensure there will be no parliamentary or logistical impediments that might detract from your remarks."

What will be interesting is the fallout from John Boehner suddenly growing a set and telling the TOTUS that he gives him permission to reschedule his 'joint session' campaign speech for the following night. Look for the term 'obstructionists' to be screamed from the pulpits of punditdom and Jay Carney's office over this slight against the Anointed One. Yet as Boehner points out in his letter, a Resolution is required to be passed by both Houses before an agreement can be made to receive the President – and Harry Reid himself said that they will not be in session until 6:30 PM on the 7th and no time for voting for that resolution.

Still, expect this regime and the media mouthpieces of the MSM to try and capitalize on the Constitutional ignorance of their audience and constituencies.

But I'd bet dollars of debt that even Obama's constituencies are going to be watching the NFL as opposed to TOTUS on the evening of the 8th.

UPDATE: <u>media reporting the White House will 'accept' Boehner's change of date</u> advice.
Oh goodie, look for The One and the State-Foisted Media to use this 'acceptance' as a pointer to insist that Obama can "compromise" with the GOP and therefore, because His Heinous has bent the knee and relented on the date he demands an audience with a joint session of Congress – everyone should "compromise" and agree with his "jobs plan".

The more hope and change, the more things stay the same with this regime, and worse for the rest of the nation.

AUTHOR: While micro-blogs such as the above have seen little online traction these past years, Alex Jones with his InfoWars has successfully created a following. And he's not alone. Others who have grown into large followings are Radix, BakedAlalska (aka Tim Treadstone), Richard Spencer, Sam Hyde, Mike Cernovich, and Milo. Then there are the up-and-comers, contenders to Fox's conservative throne, *Newsmax Media* and *Breitbart.com*.

Case in point: Alex Jones' YouTube channel where he broadcasts his show, has 1,867,224 subscribers. A mid-December broadcast dealt with the issue of U.S. Electors being lobbied to not cast their vote for President-Elect Trump. He showed a clip of the *Saturday Night Live* show skit where a Hillary impersonator shows up at an elector's front door and tries to convince her not to vote for Trump. Of course the skit was played for comedy but nonetheless, Jones points out, it is yet another attempt by which mass media tried to influence their audience in unprecedented maneuvers, some would call a coup attempt, when it came to the 2016 presidential election in our country.

Watch SNL skit on Alex Jones' Info Wars: https://www.youtube.com/watch?v=TlA_0atGpyU

On a related Alex Jones segment on his *Info Wars* show, he discusses how censorship and totalitarian authority is attempting to clasp ever more tightly onto our society. He cites as an example Germany's new law to fine its citizens €500 for criticizing/ critiquing Islam.

Alex Jones on Info Wars, 1st Amendment Under Siege December 18, 2016 :
https://www.youtube.com/watch?v=55vvu5B-BCA

And also about the Communist Chinese influence on trying to purge the 1st Amendment in the U.S.
Alex Jones, the Alex Jones Channel: https://www.youtube.com/watch?v=7yQePoRh8Rk

AUTHOR: Say, and think, what you will about the different elements of micro-media and the coalitions they represent, but keep in mind that these are what allow for a cacophony of voices. In a republic, this very cacophony of voices is what ensures the democratic process, where all concerns can be voiced and heard.

The flip-side of that is if only one or two behemoth voices are heard. Some predict that this is what is in store for our us in America and even as a global trend as we sally forth into 2017 and beyond ..

I once read an anecdote where a Democracy was described as two wolves and a sheep sitting down at table, deciding what to eat for dinner. For a further exploration into this inquiry, please see the Glossary terms at the end of the book, particularly the definitions of Democracy and Republic.

2017 Is Going To Be A Bloodbath – Confessions of a Beleaguered Independent Publisher, by Lucia Moses, *Digiday,* December 23, 2016

http://digiday.com/publishers/2017s-going-bloodbath-confessions-beleaguered-independent-publisher/

Surviving as a digital publisher is hard enough, but it's even more so for independent, pure-play digital media companies that don't have massive scale or other business lines to lean on. For the latest installment in our anonymous Confessions series, we talk to an exec at an independent publisher who worries about making it in a world where most of the ad dollars are going to Google and Facebook.

What worries you the most as an independent publisher these days?
This duopoly is essentially killing publishing. There's a Faustian bargain we've all entered into because the platforms are responsible for our livelihood but they're using our content to shore up their dominant position of owning all the data, owning all the audience. You add in Snap, it's another 5 percent. Amazon, it's another 5 percent. You're looking at an increasingly smaller slice of the pie. Brands that are independent that aren't well funded or are running out of that cash will be squeezed.

What's most frustrating about working with Facebook?
They're forcing publishers to pay for sponsored content. It's definitely an added pressure. If it's great content, it should be surfaced. Facebook is playing the same card that Google did where they released the same stream of tweaks to its algorithm, to get [brands] to buy traffic through SEM.

When it comes to their dealings with publishers, it also seems like the platforms have picked their favorites.
Whether it's *The New York Times* being subsidized by Facebook to pay for content or the Snapchat Discover kind of exclusivity, there's no rhyme or reason other than some sort of favoritism that's handed down for no reason. The randomness of the favored child is that challenge.

What else do you worry about?
The cost structure of digital display. The agencies are requiring 100 percent viewability. So if we sell a $10 CPM and deliver 70 percent viewability, which is the best you're going to be able to do, that takes your $10 CPM and moves it to a $6 CPM. Display as a whole has really shrunk as a result of viewability. 2017's going to be a bloodbath for independent publishers.

AUTHOR: So if the frigid and over-controlling advertising market response to diversity of thought, a cacophony of voices, and freedom of speech is not chilling enough, brace yourselves, because the government has now just gotten in further on the act of clamping down on 'propaganda.' As one of the Obama administrations last acts, it oversaw the successful passage of a bill in December 2016, now being referred to as the Propaganda Bill. Only cursory details are below, so the reader is highly encouraged to research and educate themselves further on this newly enacted bill that most certainly

114

can be implemented to clamp down on freedom of speech in ways that are heretofore unprecedented in our country's history.

Propaganda Bill passes in Congress

US legislation proposes new committee to counteract Russian 'covert influence', *The Guardian*, by Spencer Ackerman and Julian Borger, November 30, 2016
Source: https://www.theguardian.com/us-news/2016/nov/30/sweeping-us-laws-targeting-russian-interference-could-ensnare-trump

Obama signs defense bill establishing anti-propaganda center, *Democracy Now*, **Headlines, Dec 27 2016**

Source:https://www.democracynow.org/2016/12/27/headlines/obama_signs_defense_bill_establishing_anti_propaganda_center

President Obama on Friday signed the National Defense Authorization Act, or NDAA, providing nearly $619 billion for war and military spending. The measure passed both houses of Congress with a veto-proof majority …

Meanwhile, press freedom advocates are raising alarm over a little-known bill rolled into the NDAA, which will create a national anti-propaganda center.

Under the **Countering Disinformation and Propaganda Act**, the State Department will actively work to "recognize, understand, expose, and counter foreign state and non-state propaganda and disinformation efforts aimed at undermining United States national security interests."

AUTHOR: Robert Parry's *Consortium News* is another under-trafficked news site that is dedicated to reporting truth and facts. In order to better formulate a clear picture of what's going on in our political landscape today, it is essential reading. His author bio on the website reads as follows: "Investigative reporter Robert Parry broke many of the Iran-Contra stories for *The Associated Press* and *Newsweek* in the 1980s. You can buy his latest book, America's Stolen Narrative (available widely)."

The following is the kind of analysis characteristic of his investigative reporting style:

Pulling a J. Edgar Hoover on Trump, by Robert Parry, *Consortium News*, January 12, 2017
Source: https://consortiumnews.com/2017/01/12/pulling-a-j-edgar-hoover-on-trump/

…Trump has denounced the story as "fake news" and it is certainly true that the juicy details – reportedly assembled by a former British MI-6 spy named Christopher Steele – have yet to check out. But the placement of the rumors in a U.S. government document gave the mainstream media an excuse to publicize the material.

It's also allowed the media to again trot out the Russian word "compromat" as if the Russians invented the game of assembling derogatory information about someone and then using it to discredit or blackmail the person.

In American history, legendary FBI Director J. Edgar Hoover was infamous for using his agency to develop negative information on a political figure and then letting the person know that the FBI had the dirt and certainly would not want it to become public – if only the person would do what the FBI wanted, whether that was to reappoint Hoover to another term or to boost the FBI's budget or – in the infamous case of civil rights leader Martin Luther King – perhaps to commit suicide...

...Now, we are seeing what looks like a new phase in this "stop (or damage) Trump" strategy, the inclusion of anti-Trump dirt in an official intelligence report that was then leaked to the major media.

Whether this move was meant to soften up Trump or whether the intelligence community genuinely thought that the accusations might be true and deserved inclusion in a report on alleged Russian interference in U.S. politics or whether it was some combination of the two, we are witnessing a historic moment when the U.S. intelligence community has deployed its extraordinary powers within the domain of U.S. politics. J. Edgar Hoover would be proud...

AUTHOR: Never has there been a time more important in the history of our country than today for each citizen to allow themselves to think and speak freely. This great heritage, built into the foundations of our Constitution and our country as envisioned by our esteemed Founding Fathers, rests squarely on each individual's shoulders today. Young and old, from every race, religion, gender, age group and socio-economic strata, it is imperative that we accept the responsibility to think, speak and act for ourselves, without fear of punishment or reprisals.

When any one group of us, if even one individual, shirks from their duty, we are all weakened and diminished. A republic calls for a cacophony of voices. There are always voices that each of us would prefer not to listen to nor even, perhaps, to hear. But as has been illustrated here in this book and in hundreds upon hundreds of important treatises written by the foremost thought-leaders of their and our times, the only way a people can be and live freely, the only way the democratic process can persist in a nation founded on the principles of a republic, is for each and every one of us to think and speak freely. And above all to listen to one another, without obligation to agree or to comply with any expressed opinions or beliefs. In other words, freedom of speech, thought and expression in all its diversity is what a true republic requires and what it is founded upon.

Glossary of Terms

Alt-Right – all news media (according to liberals) that is outside of the *NYT, WaPo, LA Times, USA Today, NBC, ABC, CNN, CBS, MSNBC, Bloomberg* echo chamber; example of an "alt-right platform" as self-described by former CEO Stephen Bannon is *Breitbart News;* alt-right media examples are *Info Wars* and Radix Journal; among alt-right media stars is vocal Tweeter Mike Cernovich @Cernovich and podcaster Milo Yiannopoulos (iTunes); for a sampling, read more here:
http://www.radixjournal.com/journal/2016/12/31/the-alt-right-the-american-resistance

Banksters – a modern form of unscrupulous banker, borne out of The City (London's financial center), who, when their shenanigans cause whole economies to crash, usually make off with hundreds of $$ millions or $$billions and get off scot-free; also see gangster

CNN – Clinton News Network aka Corporate News Network

Conservatives – blue collar, uneducated, Bible belt Americans (according to the liberal elite media); see also synonyms for racist, misogynist et al (again, according to liberals)

Democracy – sometimes referred to as "rule of the majority". (literally "rule of the commoners"), in modern usage, is a system of government in which the citizens exercise power directly or elect representatives from among themselves to form a governing body, such as a parliament. According to political scientist Larry Diamond, democracy consists of four key elements: (a) A political system for choosing and replacing the government through free and fair elections; (b) The active participation of the people, as citizens, in politics and civic life; (c) Protection of the human rights of all citizens, and (d) A rule of law, in which the laws and procedures apply equally to all citizens.

Per Merriam-Webster Dictionary:
1. a: government by the people; especially: rule of the majority

b: a government in which the supreme power is vested in the people and exercised by them directly or indirectly through a system of representation usually involving periodically held free elections

2: a political unit that has a democratic government

Deplorables – American citizens who continue to have a deep and abiding love and respect for their country and who are willing to work hard to make it great again; Americans who stand and sing the national anthem at football games

Double down – a term or verb used when members of a certain reality-bubble amp up their echo chamber diatribes in order to reassure themselves that the only opinions and viewpoints that have any merit are their own

117

Echo chamber – a term or verb used when the elite liberal media speak only amongst themselves and repeat each other's PC opinions leading to the false assumption that everyone shares their opinions

Fake News – a highly subjective label used by various members of the media, politics and the public when describing either absolutely outlandish news stories that were once reserved exclusively for tabloid publications like the *Enquirer,* or when referring to stories published by news sources that differ from one's own dogmatic beliefs and opinions; see also Native Ads and Sponsored Content

Hackers – weapons of mass disruption

Info wars – 1. this is the name of the news site online (InfoWars.com) and on Youtube hosted by Alex Jones; 2. The term info wars also refers to the concept of competing factual representations of events, subjects and people in order to sway a group of people to your point of view. 'Propaganda' is the term that was most often used historically for this type of doctoring up of reports about people/places/events. (*Note the Alex Jones show, as referenced in defintion #1 above, attempts to fight against this kind of one-sided propaganda that is evident in much of mainstream liberal media today by airing differing points of view and facts that may have been obfuscated by the MSM).

Left-wing – another term for Liberals; see also liberals

Liberals – Everyone who is not necessarily hetero, white and/or Christian (according to the liberal elite media)

Liberal Elite Media – large pockets of these creatures are to be found in NY and California, but also Chicago and DC; the more liberal-leaning of these can be found in the upper echelons of corporate-owned media such as editors, publishers and owners.

Mainstream Media – corporate-owned lamestream media

MSM – see above "mainstream media"

Native Ads – a term used to refer to fake news; advertorials; advertising content made to look like and presented as editorial content (see also Sponsored Content, Fake News)

Normalize – (aka: new normal) When a collective group-think imposes its world view on reality and everyone living in its reality bubble. Ex: Kim Kardashian's penchant for posting nude selfies all over social media turned this big-butt behavior into America's new normal. And whether you agreed with this kind of behavior from a woman/wife/mother was irrelevant to whether you were expected to accept it as the "new normal." (According to the liberal media).

Obfuscate – a verb used to refer to the end result of what the news, churned out by the MSM, does to current issues relevant to the American public

Post-factual – a term used most often by former ad executives and lawyers now masquerading as members of the elite liberal media when referring to a concept for which the rest of us quite simply use the word 'lies'

Reality Bubble – the construct of an echo chamber; This is when a person surrounds him/herself with like minded individuals and allows for no differing opinions or dissension. It is a reality created by group think. Example: when a large group or mass of people drink poisoned Kool-Aid believing it will imbibe them with superpowers but instead they just roll over, rendered impotent, dead. See also "Jonestown." (Note: For those who don't understand the references "Jonestown" or "drinking the Kool-Aid" please look them up as it's imperative to be informed of this relatively recent historical event of mass suicide brought about by a strong personality imposing groupthink on his followers)

Republic – The United States of America is a republic. (from Latin: *res publica*) is a sovereign state or country which is organized with a form of government in which power resides in elected individuals representing the citizen body and government leaders exercise power according to the rule of law. In modern times, the definition of a republic is commonly referred to as a government which excludes a monarch.

PER Merriam-Webster dictionary:

1. a: a government having a chief of state who is not a monarch and who in modern times is usually a president (2): a political unit (as a nation) having such a form of government

b: a government in which supreme power resides in a body of citizens entitled to vote and is exercised by elected officers and representatives responsible to them and governing according to law (2):a political unit (as a nation) having such a form of government

c: a usually specified republican government of a political unit (ex: the French Fourth Republic)

Sponsored Content – a term used to refer to fake news; advertorials; advertising content made to look like and presented as editorial content (See also Native Ads, Fake News)

Appendix A

Examples of Fake News

Fake Trump News Caught in the Act

Washington Post corrects story on Russians hacking a Vermont utility

CNN Gets Caught in Cheating Scandal; CNN analyst Donna Brazile fed debate questions to Hillary Clinton.

CNN CAUGHT ALTERING FOOTAGE TO HELP RUMORS SURROUNDING HILLARY'S AILING HEALTH : cut out the part showing her stumbling and being slid into the van, leaving only the part showing her waiting by the curb, leaning on a concrete post.

Howard Stern confirms CNN Lied About Donald Trump regarding being in favor of the Iraq War

CNN's Chris Cuomo lied to viewers that it was illegal for regular citizens to possess emails obtained by WikiLeaks, but it was fine for the media.

CNN Caught Altering Trump Audio -- claiming Trump encouraged his supporters to cheat on Election Day.

CNN Caught Editing Trump Statement in order to correspond with the headline "Trump Says 'Racial Profiling' Will Stop Terror" even though Trump never once said "racial".

CNN criticizes Trump for saying that the NYC bombing was a bomb claiming Hillary handled it better and then caught editing Hillary footage of Hillary saying the same thing

CNN's Tom Foreman Caught Lying in Trump-Refugees 'Fact Check'

CNN softens the blow after Hillary gets caught in 9/11 lie

CNN caught on live TV staging a fake Anti-Trump protester interview

MSNBC Anchor Falsely Claims Fox News Had Christmas Party at Trump's D.C. Hotel

MSNBC Intelligence Analyst Perpetuated 'Fake News' to Discredit WikiLeaks

Newsweek Reporter Caught LYING About Trump Supporters Booing Late John Glenn Tries To Cover Tracks

REPORT: Woman Made False Claim That She Was Victim of Anti-Muslim Attack by Trump Supporters

Sheriff Clarke: Liberal Media Created 'Fake News' Pushing Ferguson Lie, 'Hand's Up, Don't Shoot'

From Twitter Feed: Jes Michael @JesRodriguez93 - January 2nd, 2017
@Cernovich Mike - here's a list I started with just fake Trump news. Of course we're passed the point 1 screenshot allows to show.

Food Lovers for Hillary, Paris Fundraising Event, September 2016 (screenshots)

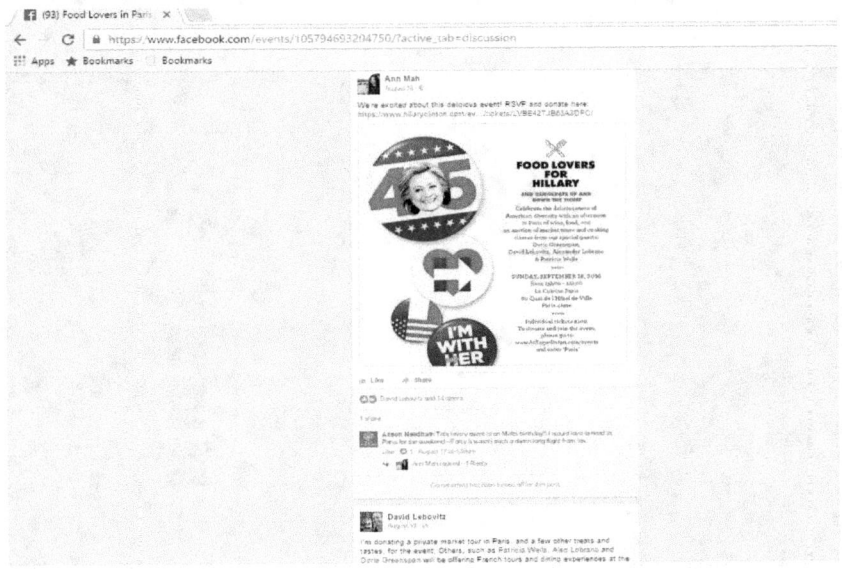

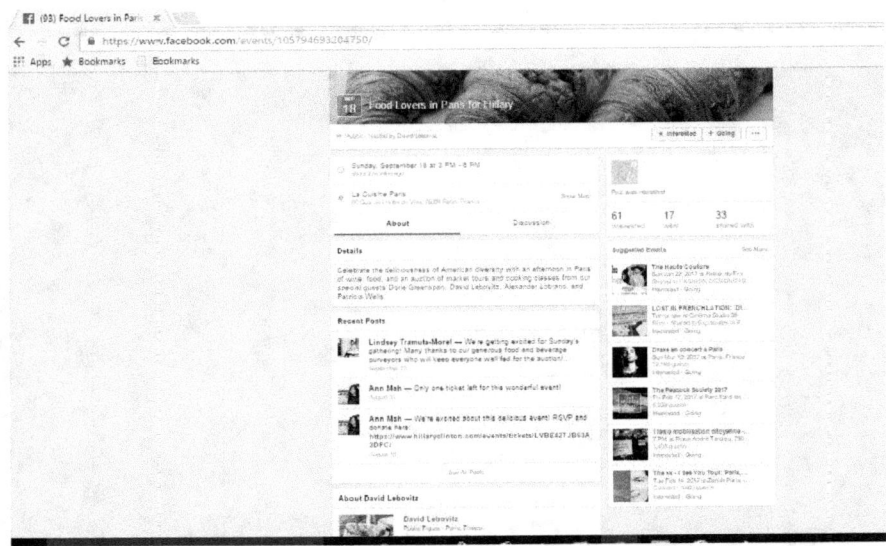

← → C 🔒 https://www.facebook.com/events/105794693204750/?active_tab=discussion

::: Apps ★ Bookmarks 🔖 Bookmarks

Photos from Art Exhibit, Cartooning for Peace, *Paris Hôtel de Ville*, Nov. 16 - January 2017
All photos copyright Paige Donner
(For complete photo slideshow please go to: *PaigeDonner.info* and click on Freedom of Speech Photos)

Appendix D

Book Cover Art, original photo copyright 2016 by Paige Donner of Original (interior) Artwork by Gérard Rancinan,

Art Gallery: Galerie Rive Gauche Marcel Strouk, located at 23, rue de Seine, Paris, Saint-Germain des Prés, 75006

Bibliography

Chapter 1 - Watchdogs of The Powerful – The Historical Role of Political Journalists

This is about the future of democracy, by Mickey Edwards, Rick Hasen, Las Vegas Review Journal editorial and the New Yorker, *USA Today, Other Views section, Opinion,* November 10, 2016)

The Fourth Estate – Essay by Stuart Pirie, Source: https://www.booksie.com/posting/stuart-pirie/the-fourth-estate-265117#k3kxpkDZooZiPYHc.99

Driving Democracy, Harvard Kennedy School, Norris, P., Chapter 8 "The Fourth Estate" 2007 pgs 1 & 2
Source: https://www.hks.harvard.edu/fs/pnorris/Acrobat/Driving%20Democracy/Chapter%208.pdf

Article 19 of the **1948 Universal Declaration of Human Rights**

Whistleblower Crackdowns, Self-Censorship, Stonewalled FOIAs: The 1st Amendment Under Attack , by Peter Van Buren, *Mother Jones,* June 2014
Source: http://www.motherjones.com/politics/2014/06/first-amendment-free-speech-attack

Times Reporter Will Not Be Called To Testify In Leak Case, by Matt Apuzzo, *New York Times,* January 12, 2015
Source: http://www.nytimes.com/2015/01/13/us/times-reporter-james-risen-will-not-be-called-to-testify-in-leak-case-lawyers-say.html?_r=0

The Role of the Media in Deepening Democracy, Coronel, S. 2003. [online]. unpan.org. Available from: Source: unpan1.un.org/intradoc/groups/public/documents/un/unpan010194.pdf

The tyranny of the fourth estate, chapter excerpt from Politics and the Media, by Jürgen Krönig, pgs.56 – 63, *Progressive Politics* Vol 3.2, June 1, 2004
Source: http://www.policy-network.net/uploadedFiles/Publications/Publications/Kronig_pn3.2%20p56-63.pdf

Taking Trump Seriously, Not Literally, by Salena Zito, *The Atlantic*, September 23, 2016
Source: http://www.theatlantic.com/politics/archive/2016/09/trump-makes-his-case-in-pittsburgh/501335/

Chapter 2 - The Insidious Hoax of An Impartial U.S. News Media

Why Independent Media?, *Democracy Now* Source: https://www.democracynow.org/about

How a Putin Fan Overseas Pushed Pro-Trump Propaganda to Americans, by Mike McIntire, *The New York Times,* December 17, 2016
Source: **http://www.nytimes.com/2016/12/17/world/europe/russia-propaganda-elections.html**

Quizzical look at campaign, from viewpoint of overseas readers, by Declan Walsh, *The New York Times* Int'l Edition November 9th, 2016 page 6

A measure of America's fever, by Declan Walsh, page 6 *NY Times* Int'l Edition November 9th 2016

Trump is Unfit For Presidency, *USA Today* Editorial Board, Sept 30 2016
Source: http://www.usatoday.com/story/opinion/2016/09/29/dont-vote-for-donald-trump-editorial-board-editorials-debates/91295020/

Vote, But Not For Trump: Our View, *USA Today*
Source: http://www.usatoday.com/story/opinion/2016/11/07/donald-trump-hillary-clinton-election-day-editorials-debates/93449852/

Soros-Funded Lefty Media Reach More Than 300 Million Every Month, Media Research Center,
Source: https://www.mrc.org/commentary/soros-funded-lefty-media-reach-more-300-million-every-month
MRC – "America's Media Watchdog"

Propaganda in America 2016, by Yoav Litvin, *CounterPunch,* November 4, 2016
Source: http://www.counterpunch.org/2016/11/04/propaganda-in-america-2016/

Chapter 3 - **The US Top Media Players by Numbers and Stats**

*All data is taken from the reported media's own official websites, unless otherwise noted.

TV Dominant News Networks
CNN, MSNBC, Fox News
http://www.journalism.org/2016/06/15/cable-news-fact-sheet/

Breitbart
https://www.similarweb.com/website/breitbart.com#overview

Washington Post
Source: http://www.capitolcommunicator.com/washington-post-circulation-drops-37-percent-since-2009-states-dcrtv/

The Atlantic Monthly
Source: https://www.theatlantic.com/past/docs/about/atlhistf.htm
Source: http://rethink.theatlantic.com/static/img/upload/pdfs/TheAtlanticMediaKit_2015.pdf

Also – **News Magazines: Fact Sheet**, by Galen Stocking, Pew Research Center, 'State of the News Media 2016', June 15, 2016
Source: http://www.journalism.org/2016/06/15/news-magazines-fact-sheet/

The Huffington Post, Buzzfeed, Vice Media
As of October 2015
http://www.ibtimes.com/huffington-posts-us-traffic-tanks-2015-buzzfeed-vice-media-grow-2142607

Democracy Now
Source: Media Research Center https://www.mrc.org/commentary/soros-funded-lefty-media-reach-more-300-million-every-month

Rush Limbaugh
Source: http://www.gossipextra.com/2016/05/26/rush-limbaugh-audience-soaring-revenues-down-5997/
& http://www.politico.com/magazine/story/2016/05/is-rush-limbaugh-in-trouble-talk-radio-213914

Univision
Source: Pew Research Center http://www.journalism.org/2016/06/15/hispanic-media-fact-sheet/

I.F. Stone Quotes, *AZ Quotes,* Source: http://www.azquotes.com/author/14178-I_F_Stone

Chapter 4 - Everything - What The Media Got Wrong About Trump's Appeal To His Electorate

They are 'taking the bait': Columnist Michael Wolff on why the media blew it on Trump, by Brian Morrissey, *Digiday* November 23, 2016
Source: http://digiday.com/publishers/digiday-podcast-michael-wolff-donald-trump/

A defiant victor tells leading TV figures they got it all wrong, by Michael M. Grynbaum and Sydney Ember, *New York Times* International Edition, November 23rd 2016
(re-printed from digital version November 21, 2016)
Source: http://www.nytimes.com/2016/11/21/business/media/trump-summons-tv-figures-for-private-meeting-and-lets-them-have-it.html?_r=0

A measure of America's fever, by Declan Walsh, *New York Times,* Int'l Edition, November 9th, 2016
(front page)

Trump v the media: did his tactics mortally would the fourth estate?, by Ed Pilkington, *The Guardian*, November 22nd 2016
Source: https://www.theguardian.com/media/2016/nov/22/election-2016-donald-trump-media-coverage?

Media warily hoping for change in Trump, by Jim Rutenberg, *New York Times* International Edition, November 15, 2016 page 9

Accomplices or antagonists: how the media handled the Trump, by Ed Pilkington, *The Guardian,* November 22, 2016 https://www.theguardian.com/us-news/2016/nov/22/journalists-media-election-2016-donald-trump

Covering Trump: An Oral History of An Unforgettable Campaign, *Columbia Journalist Review, November 22, 2016*
Source: http://www.cjr.org/special_report/trump_media_press_journalists.php
CJR's reporting team: Shelley Hepworth, Vanessa Gezari, Kyle Pope, Carlett Spike, Cory Schouten, David Uberti and Pete Vernon

Trump Won. The Media Lost. What next?, by David Folkenflik, *NPR*, November 9, 2016
Source: http://www.npr.org/2016/11/09/501460470/trump-won-the-media-lost-what-next?
Cenk Uygur Predicts Donald Trump Will Win Election 279-259, by Tim Hains, RealClearPolitics, July 31, 2016
Source:http://www.realclearpolitics.com/video/2016/07/31/cenk_uygur_predicts_donald_trump_will_w in_election_279-259.html

Chapter 5 - How Can Data-Centric Reporting Get The Data Wrong?

How did pollsters get election so wrong? By Nathan Bomey, *USA Today* November 10th 2016, News 3a

Trump Lead Widens To 2, His Biggest Yet, Despite 'November Surprise': *IBD/TIPP* Poll
Source: http://www.investors.com/politics/trump-lead-widens-to-2-his-biggest-yet-despite-november-surprise-ibdtipp-poll/

Graphs: Source:IBD/TIPP presidential election tracking poll breakdown
http://www.investors.com/politics/ibd-tipp-presidential-election-poll/

Accomplices or antagonists: how the media handled the Trump phenomenon, by Ed Pilkington, *The Guardian, November 22, 2016*
Source: https://www.theguardian.com/us-news/2016/nov/22/journalists-media-election-2016-donald-trump

Oceans of data and few facts, by Sapna Maheshwari, *New York Times* International Edition, November 15, 2016, page 8

Don't call it post-truth. There's a simpler word: lies, by Jonathan Freedland, The Guardian, December 16, 2016

Source: https://www.theguardian.com/commentisfree/2016/dec/16/not-post truth-simpler-words-lies-aleppo-trump-mainstream

Why Pollsters Got The Election So Wrong and What It Means for Marketers, by Jack Neff, *Ad Age,* November 10, 2016
Source: http://adage.com/article/campaign-trail/pollsters-wrong-means-marketers/306697/

Women who helped Trump win, by Sheryl Gay Stolberg, *NY Times* International Edition, November 14, 2016 page 5

Three Democratic Delusions, by Michael Medved, *USA Today* International Edition, December 1, 2016 page 10A

How I missed the signs of a Trump win, by Bill Sternberg, *USA Today* Opinion, November 15, 2016 page 10A (*Note: Bill Sternberg is Editor of the Editorial Page of *USA Today*)

About TIPP Source: http://www.tipponline.com/about-tipp

Chapter 6 - **Was There An Agenda? What Was It? And Why?**

They are "taking the bait": Columnist Michael Wolff on why the media blew it on Trump, by Brian Morrissey, *Digiday Podcast*, November 23, 2016
Source: http://digiday.com/publishers/digiday-podcast-michael-wolff-donald-trump/

I.F. Stone Quotes, *AZ Quotes,* Source: http://www.azquotes.com/author/14178-I_F_Stone

Donald Trump – Addressing a crowd at a gala dinner "roast" during the 2016 campaign
https://www.youtube.com/watch?v=XVPDgmJZoPM (video start time 8:02)

Unshackled Trump loses Republican support, *USA Today* International Edition, October 23, 2016 page 9A

Twitter tirade shows an unhinged candidate, *USA Today* International Edition, October 23, 2016 page 9A

Media Malpractice? Media Bias and The 2016 Election, by Tom Westervelt and Raghavan Mayur, *Investor's Business Daily,* Monday, November 21, 2016
Source: http://www.tipponline.com/news/election-2016/792-media-malpractice-media-bias-and-the-2016-election

Accomplices or antagonists: how the media handled the Trump, by Ed Pilkington, *The Guardian*, November 22, 2016

Source: https://www.theguardian.com/us-news/2016/nov/22/journalists-media-election-2016-donald-trump

Covering Trump: An Oral History of An Unforgettable Campaign, *Columbia Journalist Review,* November 22, 2016
Source: http://www.cjr.org/special_report/trump_media_press_journalists.php
CJR's reporting team: Shelley Hepworth, Vanessa Gezari, Kyle Pope, Carlett Spike, Cory Schouten, David Uberti and Pete Vernon

Trump v the media: Did his tactics mortally wound the fourth estate?, by Ed Pilkington, *The Guardian*, November 22, 2016
Source: https://www.theguardian.com/media/2016/nov/22/election-2016-donald-trump-media-coverage?

Media has itself to blame for such an epic election fail, by Michael Wolff, *USA Today*, Money 7A, November 15, 2016

Accomplices or antagonists: how the media handled the Trump phenomenon, Ed Pilkington, *The Guardian,* November 22, 2016
Source: https://www.theguardian.com/us-news/2016/nov/22/journalists-media-election-2016-donald-trump

Lies in guise of news, by Nicholas Kristof, *New York Times* International Edition, November 14, 2016 page 16 Opinion

Tommy Craggs, politics editor, Slate:
Source: https://www.theguardian.com/us-news/2016/nov/22/journalists-media-election-2016-donald-trump

Bill Clinton's 1995 State of the Union address: (C-Span)
VIDEO + transcripts https://www.c-span.org/video/?c4351026/clinton-1995-immigration-sotu

Media Malpractice? Media Bias and The 2016 Election, Written by Tom Westervelt and Raghavan Mayur, *Investor's Business Daily,* Monday, 21 November 2016
http://www.tipponline.com/news/election-2016/792-media-malpractice-media-bias-and-the-2016-election

Campaign 2016 Updates: Another newspaper that has long backed GOP candidates bucks Donald Trump, *LA Times*, Sept 29, 2016
Source: http://www.latimes.com/nation/politics/trailguide/la-na-live-updates-trailguide-don-t-vote-for-trump-says-usa-today-1475192834-htmlstory.html

Don't vote for Trump,' says *USA Today* in first presidential endorsement in its history, by Melanie Mason, *LA Times,* September 29, 2016

132

Journalists need new rules after Trump, Marc Ambinder , *USA Today*, October 31, 2016
Source: http://www.usatoday.com/story/opinion/2016/10/31/journalists-truth-facts-trump-clinton-marc-ambinder/92847348/

Media has itself to blame for such an epic election fail, by Michael Wolff, *USA Today*, Money 7A, November 15, 2016

Trump v the media: did his tactics mortally wound the fourth estate? by Ed Pilkington, *The Guardian*, November 22, 2016
Source: https://www.theguardian.com/media/2016/nov/22/election-2016-donald-trump-media-coverage

Have we been pulled into a cocoon by social media? By Jenna Wortham, *NY Times* International Edition, page 8 (printed originally in the *NY Times Magazine*)

Chapter 7 - **The Rise In Popularity of Fake News**

Evelyn Beatrice Hall, Ch. 7: Helvétius: The Contradiction(1906), p. 199. Often misattributed to Voltaire.

How Sponsored Content Is Becoming King in a Facebook World, by John Herrman, *New York Times*, July 24, 2016
Source: http://www.nytimes.com/2016/07/25/business/sponsored-content-takes-larger-role-in-media-companies.html?_r=0

Donald Trump Clung to Birther Lie for Years and Still Isn't Apologetic, by Michael Barbaro, *New York Times*, Sept. 16, 2016
source: http://www.nytimes.com/2016/09/17/us/politics/donald-trump-obama-birther.html?_r=1

ACLU - position paper on Freedom of Speech
Source: https://www.aclu.org/other/freedom-expression-aclu-position-paper

Twitter suspends major alt-right accounts, by Amar Toor, *The Verge,* November 16 2016)
Source: http://www.theverge.com/2016/11/16/13648922/twitter-suspends-alt-right-accounts-richard-spencer-trump-

Facebook, In Cross-hairs After Election, Is Said to Question Its Influence, by Mike Isaac, *New York Times* International Edition, November 12 2016

Twitter suspends several accounts in alt-right purge, by James Rogers, *Fox News*, November 17, 2016

Source: Fox News http://www.foxnews.com/tech/2016/11/17/twitter-suspends-several-accounts-in-alt-right-purge.html

Twitter Holocaust, SPLC Has Dozens of Alt-Right Accounts Deleted, Then Brags About It, by Ethan Ralph, *The Ralph Retort*, November 16, 2016
Source: http://theralphretort.com/twitter-holocaust-splc-dozens-alt-right-accounts-deleted-brags-11016016/

Twitter suspends alt-right accounts, *by Jessica Guynn, USA Today,* November 16, 2016
Source: http://www.usatoday.com/story/tech/news/2016/11/15/twitter-suspends-alt-right-accounts/93943194/

Would Facebook or Twitter Ever Ban President Trump? By Will Oremus, *Slate*, Nov 28, 2016
http://www.slate.com/articles/technology/technology/2016/11/would_facebook_or_twitter_ban_president_trump.html

Meet The CEO of GAB, The Free Speech Alternative to Twitter, by Charlie Nash, *Breitbart.com*, August 23, 2016
Source: http://www.breitbart.com/tech/2016/08/23/meet-the-ceo-of-gab-the-free-speech-alternative-to-twitter/

Freedom of Speech : Quotes Source: https://en.wikiquote.org/wiki/Freedom_of_speech

Edward R. Murrow Quote, Source:
https://www.goodreads.com/author/quotes/178884.Edward_R_Murrow

The ACLU's Position Paper
Source: https://www.aclu.org/other/freedom-expression-aclu-position-paper

Committee to Protect Journalists: President Trump would be threat to press freedom (*USA Today*, October 13, 2016)
Source: http://www.usatoday.com/story/news/politics/onpolitics/2016/10/13/committee-protect-journalists-president-trump-would-threaten-press-freedom/92002796/

Facebook shouldn't check facts, *New York Times*, International Edition, November 29th, 2016, pg. 16
Op-Ed by Jessica Lessin, founder and Chief Executive of *The Information*

US Media to Get Even After Clinton's Loss Amid Crackdown on 'Fake News' Sites, *Sputnik News,* published November 23, 2016
Source: https://sputniknews.com/world/201611231047736563-us-corporate-media-fake-news/

Fake News? It's All Fake by Bill Bonner, the Palm Beach Group Newsletter, December 23, 2016
Source: http://palmbeachgroup.com/content/palm-beach-daily/fake-news-its-all-fake/32959/

Evaluating Information : The Cornerstone of Civic Online Reasoning, by the Stanford History Education Group, published November 22, 2016

https://sheg.stanford.edu/upload/V3LessonPlans/Executive%20Summary%2011.21.16.pdf

Researchers "shocked" to find students' *in*ability to differentiate between fake and credible news, *NPR*
Source: http://www.npr.org/sections/thetwo-way/2016/11/23/503129818/study-finds-students-have-dismaying-inability-to-tell-fake-news-from-real
Evaluating Information: The Cornerstone of Civic Online Reasoning November 22, 2016
Study from January 2015 to June 2016
Source: entire study that *NPR* article is based on can be found here
https://sheg.stanford.edu/upload/V3LessonPlans/Executive%20Summary%2011.21.16.pdf

Queen Bee Michelle's 22 Staffers
http://www.snopes.com/politics/obama/firstlady.asp

Michelle Obama Has 26 Tax Payer Assistants That Make How Much!, by Lauren Richardson, Truth Uncensored, March 16, 2014
Source: http://truthuncensored.net/michelle-obama-has-26-tax-payer-funded-assistants-that-make-how-much/

Glenn Beck says First Lady Michelle Obama has 43 on her staff while Nancy Reagan had just 3, by Robert Farley, *Politifact*, March 4, 2011
Source: http://www.politifact.com/truth-o-meter/statements/2011/mar/04/glenn-beck/glenn-beck-says-first-lady-michelle-obama-has-43-h/

Queen Bee Michelle Obama Has Largest First Lady Staff, *Truth or Fiction*, updated 1/8/16
Source: https://www.truthorfiction.com/queen-bee-michelle-obama-largest-first-lady-staff-fiction/

Why Facebook Wants Its Say in the Future of Journalism, by Adam Lashinsky, *Fortune,* January 12, 2017
Source: http://fortune.com/2017/01/12/data-sheet-facebook-journalism/

Annual Report to Congress on White House Office Staff
Source: https://www.whitehouse.gov/assets/documents/July1Report-Draft12.pdf

Facebook, Google to take fake news seriously, by Jon Swartz, Jessica Guynn and Elizabeth Weise, *USA Today* International Edition, November 17, 2016 page 7A

E. Y. Harburg, the lyricist of Somewhere Over The Rainbow, song from The Wizard of Oz

Chapter 8 – **Info Wars**

Accomplices or antagonists: how the media handled the Trump phenomenon, by Ed Pilkington, *The Guardian*, November 22, 2016
Source: **https://www.theguardian.com/us-news/2016/nov/22/journalists-media-election-2016-donald-trump**

Lies in guise of news, by Nicholas Kristof, *NY Times* International Edition, Monday November 14, 2016

My Unhappy Life as a Climate Heretic, by Roger Pielke, Jr., *Wall Street Journal* European Edition, December 5, 2016

Gingrich: NY Times Guilty of 'Totally Fake,' 'Conspiratorial BS' Stories by Pam Key, December 11, 2016
Source: **http://www.breitbart.com/video/2016/12/11/gingrich-nyt-times-guilty-of-totally-fake-conspiratorial-bs-stories/**

Just How Gray Are The White Helmets of Syria?, by Jan Oberg, *Counterpunch,* November 4, 2016
Source: http://www.counterpunch.org/2016/11/04/just-how-gray-are-the-white-helmets-of-syria/

Who Are The White Helmets, by Yasmeen Serhan, *The Atlantic,* September 30, 2016
https://www.theatlantic.com/news/archive/2016/09/syria-white-helmets/502073/

The Government launches a new stabilisation support package to Iraq and Syria, *Ministry of Foreign Affairs of Denmark*, October 18, 2016
Source: http://um.dk/en/news/NewsDisplayPage/?newsID=B2AA73FB-D00D-42A1-B11E-F8E42069426D

Chapter 9 – **Can Talking Heads Become Listening Heads?**

Accomplices or antagonists: how the media handled the Trump phenomenon, Ed Pilkington, *The Guardian,* November 22, 2016
Source: **https://www.theguardian.com/us-news/2016/nov/22/journalists-media-election-2016-donald-trump**   from original source:
http://www.cjr.org/special_report/trump_media_press_journalists.php

How Donald Trump's press steak fake-out sends a scary sign to media, by Marcus Gilmer, Mashable, November 16, 2016
http://mashable.com/2016/11/16/trump-dodges-reporters-again/#94jLCGKll8qW

Martin Luther and the printing press, by Patrick Kramer, *info age*, September 29, 2011
http://patrickkramer.umwblogs.org/2011/09/29/martin-luther-and-the-printing-press/

Obama's Legacy, An Abundance of Executive Actions, by Clyde Wayne Crews Jr., *Forbes*, January 10, 2016
Source: http://www.forbes.com/sites/waynecrews/2016/01/10/this-inventory-of-obamas-dozens-of-executive-actions-frames-his-final-state-of-the-union-address/#1381579641bc

The number of executive orders by every U.S. President, by Amrita Khalid, *The Daily Dot*, June 13 2016 later updated on December 20 2016
Source for below: http://www.dailydot.com/layer8/number-of-executive-orders-per-president/

Full Data Graph on all U.S. Presidential executive orders by numbers.
http://www.presidency.ucsb.edu/data/orders.php

Presidential Executive Orders and Executive Memoranda, from The Competitive Enterprise Institute, *Ten Thousand Commandments,* Chapter 3, May 3, 2016
Source: https://cei.org/10KC/Chapter-3

Graph Source: http://www.forbes.com/sites/waynecrews/2016/01/10/this-inventory-of-obamas-dozens-of-executive-actions-frames-his-final-state-of-the-union-address/#1381579641bc

Reality Check: How Obama Has Actually Issued More Executive Action Than Any President in Modern History, by Ben Swann, *Truth In Media*, January 26, 2016
Source: http://truthinmedia.com/reality-check-obama-actually-issued-exec-action-president-modern-history/

Source for cited Exec Order: **The White House,** https://www.whitehouse.gov/the-press-office/removing-barriers-responsible-scientific-research-involving-human-stem-cells

Source for cited excerpted quote: **The Embryo Project,** https://embryo.asu.edu/pages/barack-obama-executive-order-13505-november-2008

Fellow Trump Critics Maybe Try a Little Listening, by David Brooks Op-Ed article *New York Times* :
Source: http://www.nytimes.com/2016/11/22/opinion/fellow-trump-critics-maybe-try-a-little-listening.html

Chapter 10 – **Going Forward – In A Democracy With A Broken Fourth Estate, What Role Does Media Take?**

William E. Borah, remarks in the Senate (April 19, 1917), Congressional Record, vol. 55, p. 837.
Source: https://en.wikiquote.org/wiki/Freedom_of_speech

Trump v the media: did his tactics mortally wound the fourth estate? by Ed Pilkington, *The Guardian,* November 22, 2016
Source: **https://www.theguardian.com/media/2016/nov/22/election-2016-donald-trump-media-coverage**

Accomplices or antagonists: how the media handled the Trump phenomenon, Ed Pilkington, *The Guardian,* November 22, 2016
Source: **https://www.theguardian.com/us-news/2016/nov/22/journalists-media-election-2016-donald-trump** from original source:
http://www.cjr.org/special_report/trump_media_press_journalists.php

China's media casts U.S. As dysfunctional by Chris Buckley, *New York Times* International Edition, December 16, 2016

Donald Trump's win means the biased media needs to change, by Michael Goodwin, *NY Post,* November 13, 2016
Source: **http://nypost.com/2016/11/13/donald-trumps-win-means-the-biased-media-needs-to-change/**

Advertisers pulling ads from Breitbart, by Shareen Pathak, *Digiday,* November 22, 2016
http://digiday.com/brands/brands-pulling-ads-placed-breitbart/

Amid backlash, Twitter vows to crack down on hate speech, by Jessica Guynn, *USA Today* International Edition, November 7, 2016, Money 7A

Mainstream Media's Reputation Currently Broken, by Kathleen Parker, *Newsmax Media,* November 20, 2016
Source: **http://www.newsmax.com/KathleenParker/trump-journalism-political-media/2016/11/20/id/759851/**

Zuckerberg and Facebook must defend truth, By Jim Rutenberg, *New York Times* International Edition, November 22, 2016

Breitbart declares war on Kellogg's after brand pulls advertising, by Shareen Pathak November 30, 2016
Source: **http://digiday.com/brands/breitbart-calls-boycott-kelloggs-brand-pulls-advertising/**

IJR's Alex Skatell: Media is now about loyalists, by Brian Morrissey, *Digiday Podcast*, January 4, 2017 (*IJR is Independent Journal Review)
Source: http://digiday.com/publishers/ijrs-alex-skatell-media-now-loyalists/

The Rubin Report, A talk show about big ideas and free speech. Hosted by Dave Rubin.
http://www.rubinreport.com/about#crew
Hosted on the platform: **https://www.patreon.com/rubinreport**

In a world of fake news, real journalism must be paid for, by Mark Thompson, *The Guardian* Media Opinion, December 16 2016
Source: https://www.theguardian.com/commentisfree/2016/dec/16/fake-news-journalism-digital? CMP=share_btn_link

The Information's Jessica Lessin: Facebook media relations will worsen, by Brian Morrissey, Digiday Podcast, January 11, 2017
Source: http://digiday.com/publishers/the-information-jessica-lessin-digiday-podcast/

Trump's attacks on the press may save it, by Jim Rutenberg, *The New York Times* International Edition, Tuesday December 20, 2016, page 10

About Advance Publications, *Columbia Journalism Review,* **http://www.cjr.org/resources/? c=advance**

These Fifteen Billionaires Own America's News Media Companies, by Kate Vinton, *Forbes*, June 1, 2016
Source: http://www.forbes.com/sites/katevinton/2016/06/01/these-15-billionaires-own-americas-news-media-companies/#4232f2f330b4

I.F. Stone's Weekly, The Website of I.F. Stone, Source: **http://www.ifstone.org/weekly.php**

About First Look Media, First Look Media, Source: *https://firstlook.media/jobs/*

Glenn Greenwald, *The Intercept*, Source: https://theintercept.com/staff/glenn-greenwald/

The Audacity of An Arrogant Despot, A Micro-blog - *Sword At the Ready,* September 2011
Source: https://swordattheready.wordpress.com/2011/09/01/the-audacity-of-an-arrogant-despot/

1st Amendment Under Siege, by Alex Jones on *Info Wars,* December 18, 2016
https://www.youtube.com/watch?v=55vvu5B-BCA

2017 Is Going To Be A Bloodbath – Confessions of a Beleaguered Independent Publisher, by Lucia Moses, *Digiday,* December 23, 2016

http://digiday.com/publishers/2017s-going-bloodbath-confessions-beleaguered-independent-publisher/

US legislation proposes new committee to counteract Russian 'covert influence', *The Guardian*, by Spencer Ackerman and Julian Borger, November 30, 2016

Source: **https://www.theguardian.com/us-news/2016/nov/30/sweeping-us-laws-targeting-russian-interference-could-ensnare-trump**

Obama signs defense bill establishing anti-propaganda center, *Democracy Now*, Headlines, Dec 27 2016
Source:https://www.democracynow.org/2016/12/27/headlines/obama_signs_defense_bill_establishing_

Pulling a J. Edgar Hoover on Trump, by Robert Parry, *Consortium News*, January 12, 2017
Source: https://consortiumnews.com/2017/01/12/pulling-a-j-edgar-hoover-on-trump/

Author Bio

Paige Donner has written for the *New York Times*, the *Los Angeles Times, Variety, Huffington Post, Fodor's* Guidebooks and *USA Today*, among others. She is an Alaska-born, California/Hawaii-raised journalist. Since moving back to Paris in 2010, she has specialized in being a media entrepreneur as well as photo, travel and lifestyle journalism. Prior to that, she lived in Los Angeles where she was a journalist, screenwriter and filmmaker.

She has one novel published, *I'll Take Paris*, is editing a second novel and at work on a third. You can listen to her podcast, Paris GOOD food + wine, on iTunes and download her Apps, Paris Food And Wine, The Podcast Channel Network and Bordeaux Food & Wine for iOS and Android.

She shares her Paris apartment with the best dog in the world, a rescue aptly named *Idéale*.